"Bea… touch the soul with…

Tim Freke, Author – *The Mystery Experience,* and *Jesus & The Lost Goddess* (co-authored with Peter Gandy)

"A beautiful collection of poems that ring with the wonder of self-discovery. The inner seeing and mystical perception of life are conveyed with refreshing authenticity, depth and a unique voice and flow. C.W. Blackburn brings great sensitivity and richness to his attempt to give expression to that which exists before words. The collection is an exploration into Being that delights the heart and will certainly resonate with seekers and lovers of Truth."

Shruti Bakshi, Author and Poet – *HeartWords: Mystic Poems*

"A highly engaging, absorbing volume with a great variety of subject matter and a diversity of expression and emotion. The poems are lyrical and rhythmic, like a series of songs, and the work is deeply felt and embraces universal truth effortlessly and without pretence or strain. There is an evocative sense of time and the past in these poems, and a wistful contemplation of eternity. Even the more internal and cerebral poems are linked to the physicality of places and the elements. Some of the most successful poems are the shortest and simplest. *Roots* catches beautifully the theme of eternity that underpins many of the poems. *The Stranger, Whole* and *Sea-Horses* create potent pictures and atmospheres. *Fragments* is enormously powerful and deeply melodic. However, the poem which distils all of Blackburn's themes and concerns is the deceptively simple *Doors* – a really superb piece of work. These poems are unshowy and unpretentious, with no spurious attempt to make them modern or experimental. Throughout the collection, Blackburn takes us on an evolving journey of mental storms, full of release, self-doubt and self-realisation which, finally, despite everything, is life-affirming."

John Foster, Playwright and Screenwriter

"Unique and magical, C.W. Blackburn's poems have a distinctive way of capturing the essence of his awakening journey. In his writing, the mind is taken outside of the normality of linear speech into the quantum world of words in a powerful and activating way. The more you submerge yourself in this expansive experience, the more it will open your heart."

Samantha SolBright Rodriguez, Author – *Living as Pure Love: Returning To Our True Essence*

"Thank you, C.W. Blackburn! I have spent the past couple of months journeying with your stunning words. You are truly a shaman who has traversed the underworld, returning with wisdom – and poetry – for the benefit of many beings. You have a great gift for sinking our hearts 'into the margins of forever.' Bowing in gratitude."

Rashani Réa, Author – *Beyond Brokenness,* and *Go Slowly, Breathe and Smile* (co-authored with Thich Nhat Hanh)

Published in the United Kingdom by Sundara Poetry Press.

Cover art by Stefan Armoneit

Cover design by Adam McKillop

ISBN: 978-1-7397728-0-2

Where Words Are Yet To Be Spoken:

Poems for Presence

C.W. Blackburn

Sundara Poetry Press

'There is only one step on the journey,
And that is the step into yourself…'

For William, 1938 – 2020.
I'm sorry I wasn't there.
This is what I was doing.

Acknowledgements

To everyone who dared to celebrate the gift of being alive or followed a dream; who questioned themselves and found a more authentic way to be; who achieved something true, even when the world was against them.

To everyone who performed a kindness in place of a wrong; who looked at another with understanding and compassion; who gave someone hope, instead of despair.

To everyone who let the beauty of life move them; who gave their love freely, confident in their own heart and their power to give; who looked at this world, full of fear and anger, and wanted to make it a better place.

To everyone who spoke out against injustice and discrimination; who looked at our diversity through the eyes of equality; who was unafraid to be themselves, self-assured in their own individuality and strength.

To everyone who strived to live with simplicity and humbleness; who respected this planet and the mysterious wonder of nature; who wanted to leave something to be enjoyed for the generations to come.

To everyone who was patient and calm in the face of adversity; who remained pure in their heart when everything seemed lost; who looked into the darkness, and smiled.

For the misfits, non-conformists, eccentrics and dreamers – the loners, romantics, artists and rebels.

To everyone who defied the odds and lived their love fearlessly.

This book is for you.

Thank you.

Contents

Foreword

The language of the soul is unmistakable to those who know it, to those who have been initiated into its intricacies. This initiation into the mystical comes in many ways, nearly all of them involving periods of struggle punctuated by moments of grace, respite, and insight. Despite the myriad forms such initiations take – each one being unique to the individual – the language borne out of them has a flavour of its own. It is the lingua franca of the divine. To say so is not to claim that those who speak this language are in themselves divine or special; it is simply to say that they have spent time in the mystical realms, and they have returned bearing poetic gifts.

My first encounter with C.W. Blackburn – before we had spoken – was via the poems in this collection. I was immediately struck by a sense of recognition, a deep knowing of what his words convey, his language unequivocally mystical. Poetry is, of course, the natural language of the mystic, but C.W. is not only a mystic who writes poetry; he is also a consummate poet, steeped in the English poetic tradition. His love of poetry as an art form shines through his words, and he wholeheartedly acknowledges those who have come before him. Like poets such as Keats and Wordsworth, he effortlessly evokes the despair and delicacies of the human condition and, like them, the beauty and simplicity of the countryside in which he resides is central to his poetry. Nature is everywhere in these pages; crows, dark night skies, grass, waves, oaks, larks, sparrows, dandelions, the dawn light. We cannot help but be with him on the beaches and in the fields of the English south coast. The earth, in all her bounty, embraces his every move. His wonder at the miraculousness of existence – that any of this exists at all – is never far from the surface. As he says in *Pythia*,

What mystery,
That I should be here at all –

C.W.'s poetry is not, I should note, a poetry of escape or fantasy. He does not sugar-coat the pain and suffering that so often form part of the fabric of a human life. Rather, his is a poetry of deep immersion. He is alive and present to the richness and nuance not just of the outer world, but also to his vibrant inner world, to the teeming life of the soul and to the frequently tempestuous life of the psyche, with all its neuroses and fears. In *Essences* he tells us,

I want to release what keeps me bound,
To live unfolding the whole spectrum.

In my understanding, it is this willingness to live the whole spectrum that opens the door to what lies beyond our neuroses and fears. It is not a matter of healing or transcending the struggles of human existence – although there may well be moments of healing and transcendence – but rather of venturing into the space of the mystical, to the liminal space where words are yet to be spoken. This place has tangible qualities; down or under rather than up, inner rather than outer, dark rather than light. Initially forbidding or even terrifying, a while spent there begins to attune the senses to a different kind of reality. C.W.'s evocative description of it in *Hope* chimes perfectly with my own experience:

If you want to know where I've been,
I went under, I went within –
To a place that's not on any maps,
For a time no clocks can measure.

In this place of paradox, where soul-rending heartbreak sits side by side with bittersweet love and breath-taking grace, we begin to learn how to be. As we do so, we begin to reconnect to something we thought we had lost. It goes by many names; presence is perhaps the simplest. Coming back into contact with presence brings us back into contact with the reality of ourselves and the world; it can be both exhilarating and profoundly disorientating to be removed from our everyday consciousness. Yet in those moments there is an undeniable sense of stillness, grace, and the presence of something in addition to ourselves. In those moments, we are no longer alone in our struggles, and we see that we are so much more than the wretched or broken creatures that we often take ourselves to be. As C.W. says in *Scream*,

Quite simply, my friend –
You are a masterpiece,
Waiting to happen.

In the process we become, as C.W. so beautifully puts it in *The Way of Love*, witnesses for our own hearts. A sweetness and tenderness towards life, ourselves, and others begins, little by little, to permeate our experience. This tenderness invites us to let go of the tight grip that we have on so many aspects of life. There is a natural process of falling away or coming undone; this is not something that one does, but something that starts to happen seemingly of its own accord. As C.W. describes it in *Freak*:

I used to cling so tightly to how I was seen.
At the mercy of other minds. Lost in the particulars.

Now I'm letting it all fall away.

These poetic offerings touch us, the reader, in unexpected places. Moments of sweetness and grace emerge as we read. We might smile, or well up, or feel a sense of resonance. These are poems of remembrance, longing, and celebration. They invite us to step into the mysteries and depths of life. They are, without doubt, poems for the soul, and I am very thankful for them.

Fiona Robertson
Author of *The Dark Night of the Soul: A Journey from Absence to Presence*
November 2021

Preface

The poems in this collection were written over a five year period, between 2016 - 2021. The majority were written during a time in which mental health difficulties I had struggled with since my teenage years resurfaced and had a significant effect on my life. I started writing again as a form of self-therapy, to help me re-connect with something I sensed I had lost – a feeling that was with me in my earlier years but had long since been buried under the pressure of my more worldly concerns.

At the age of fourteen, I was diagnosed with obsessive-compulsive disorder, a condition which haunted me for the duration of my teenage years. Although I thought I had managed to get this affliction under control by the time I reached my early twenties, as a result of the anxiety I also started to suffer from panic attacks, which varied in their severity from mild to extreme. In 2016, after a period in which the attacks had seemed to decline, they returned and threatened to overwhelm me, physically and mentally. The smallest occurrences could trigger an attack, sending waves of apprehension and unease through my body, leaving me feeling weak, alone, and vulnerable.

It was during this time that I started meditating again, a practice I had engaged with in my early twenties when I developed an interest in Buddhism and spirituality, but had subsequently given up on to try and focus on matters that seemed more important, like career and relationships. As I continued to relax into the space and silence that the meditation created, I started coming back to something that felt more real within myself. One evening, whilst meditating, I began to sense a familiar energy passing through me, one that I had not felt for years. It had a quality that was both new and old at the same time – a sensation that was very close to my heart, and yet greater than me in some undefinable way. Although I had lost it in the intervening years, I recognised that this presence had always been there with me, spontaneously arising at certain other moments in my life – falling in love, walking in nature, contemplating the stars.

I started to question if this presence I was now feeling was more 'me' than the person I had thought I was, the one who had allowed himself to become so restricted and confined by his fear and anxiety. From there, I began to wonder: if this was true, how could I centre myself in this presence more permanently? What would it mean to truly heal, given that the task of changing my perception after a lifetime of worry and doubt seemed so insurmountable? I knew there was a wall of illusion constantly appearing in my mind, and if I wanted to break through it, I had to find a way to transform my vision. I looked around the room and realised I'd been so lost in the misconceptions of my mind that I wasn't truly inhabiting that space anymore

– like I was drifting in a dream. Acknowledging that feeling, everything in the room took on a lucid quality, like the air was full of the most ethereal light. That's when the voice of intuition whispered within me and said I should start writing my poems again, another practice I had engaged with years before and given up on, assuming that I wasn't talented or interesting or creative enough to pursue further.

At that point, I hadn't written for years, so I sat down with a dictionary and tried an automatic writing technique I had toyed with previously. I flicked through the pages and wrote down words at random, just going with the flow – whatever felt right. Suddenly, that artistic channel I had known and delighted in years before opened again, and the result was *Yields* – a strange, abstract poem that only later started to reveal a hidden message in its meaning.

Continuing to identify with this artistic, sensitive side turned out to have a surprising effect on me. The hard times didn't go away – in truth, I kept sinking further and further down – but my poetry gave me a means of exploring my thoughts and feelings that began a slow process of healing at a deeper level of being – a return to an inner-power that I desperately needed to keep me stable on a day-to-day basis. I started to re-explore an imaginative, spiritual dimension in my mind that seemed to take me down an endless rabbit hole of realisation and contemplation – and from that darkness, occasionally, a new poem would emerge. Some came to me through thoughts and dreams, others from spontaneous rumination on the spiritual texts and poetry I had been engaging with. They all felt channeled, to a certain degree. Sometimes I didn't even understand the idea until I had written the first draft. And over time, my poetic voice began to take on multiple dimensions that slowly convinced me there is more hidden in the human consciousness than the 'ordinary world' we catch sight of in the mind's reflection.

Indeed, the greatest experience life could offer me during this time turned out not to be anything I could do, but rather, living within the context in which all experience takes place. To me, this knowing isn't of the gross and physical kind – it is mysterious and metaphysical. It is the open space of awareness – the length and breadth of an ever-deepening vision that is able to assimilate experience at higher levels of presence and express them in new and unexpected ways. It is the stillness where the voice can find its authenticity and grace. It is the quiet and calm outside of the mundane. In its essence, it is the silence – where words are yet to be spoken.

It is in this spirit that I offer you these poems.

Introduction

The poems in this book were originally conceived of as three separate collections, but when the thought first came to me to publish them, it seemed right that they should sit together as one work, tracking the course of my artistic development, which unfolded alongside my spiritual explorations and my struggles with mental health. I knew that when gathered together, I wanted each collection to be separated as originally intended, and that I would therefore need an over-arching title to unite them as one book. With that in mind, I have chosen *Where Words Are Yet To Be Spoken*, the last line from one of my earliest poems, to collect them under – a title that is both personal to my experience and, at the same time, universal to the spirit they were written in.

And what is that spirit? What is this presence? If I had to put it into words, I would say: in presence, we are aware of a deeper dimension of consciousness – one that transcends and yet encompasses our everyday personality, with all of its learned habits of thought and feeling. In presence, we experience the truth and beauty of Being – a degree of awareness known for its perfect contentment, ecstasy, and bliss. In presence, the heart transcends the mind and we become at one with the love that is the essential quality of our consciousness, perceiving the inherent divinity of creation – the abundance and mystery that both surrounds us and lies within, waiting to be realised. This is not the way that we usually see the world by any means – and yet, this vision does come to us by its own grace in rare and exceptional moments.

When I look back, I recognise this presence was there with me in my childhood and teenage years, though largely unawakened. It wasn't until my early twenties that I had my first conscious experience of it, stood alone in a field in Keswick, watching the shadows of clouds moving over the surrounding mountains and fells. At that moment, something powerful and euphoric came into my awareness and I realised for the first time, outside of any intellectualisation, what the poets must mean when they talk about eternity. Indeed, for me, 'eternity' is not a concept or abstract idea, but a felt experience – a perfect alignment with the present moment, which is both fleetingly small and yet large enough to contain everything within it. Eternity is not never-ending time, it is timelessness – the spacious and peaceful awareness of a transcendental dimension of consciousness that is absolute, changeless, and everlasting. These are big words, I know, but to me, this is not something extraordinary – it is utterly simple, completely natural – and its essential quality is that sense of happiness and abiding love we are continuously seeking in all of our endeavours.

The poems in each of the following collections were composed in awareness of this presence, which only returned to me after a period of struggle in my late twenties that forced me to re-evaluate my approach to mental health. The mind is only one aspect of our total being – which encompasses the mind, the heart, the body, and the soul – and so it seemed to me that my mental health crisis was also a spiritual health crisis – a 'dark night of the soul', to use the term popularised by Saint John of the Cross. By delving deeper into the many dimensions of that spiritual understanding, my mind slowly started to heal old wounds of its own accord, as it came into alignment with that higher transformative power through the spiritual texts and practices I engaged with. For this reason, you will find poems in this collection that touch on elements of most of the major world religions and spiritualities – Christianity, Judaism, Buddhism, Hinduism, Islam and Wicca. I have explored and respect them all – and yet, my faith and belief remain outside of any one system of thought. We share this spirit, despite our differences. It is the birth-right and inheritance of every soul. We are united by its love.

Although the three collections trace the progress of my journey and the development and evolution of this awareness, I have separated and mixed the poems that seemed to fit best together. However, they do mostly follow the linear progression in which they were written. The poems in *The Stranger* were written in 2016-2018, when I was emerging from and trying to live with the effects of a mental breakdown. The poems were composed spontaneously in those moments of elucidation and enlightenment that helped me to push past that darkness into which I had fallen, and back into a clearer headspace that was less bound by the fear and anxiety that seemed so all-consuming and overwhelming.

Everything & Forever was written during a period in 2018-2019 when I retreated from the world, almost lost in the fear and defeat. This was a chapter in my life where I spent a lot of time alone, trying to make sense of who I was and how I saw the world. For the first time, I wanted to try and grow, not by blocking out and putting a brave face on my problems, but by honouring how I felt. This began a slow and ongoing process of healing, as my mind and heart came into alignment with that spiritual sense of presence that became so important to me. It wasn't an instantaneous or miraculous revelation – but by working with the feeling of a higher power, eventually I did break through to that inner-space of freedom, faith and possibility I had lost years before, resulting in a new sense of strength and transcendence in my life and writing.

Hope and *Divinity* bring us into 2019-2021, a time of increasing uncertainty in the world, but one in which I grounded that presence and allowed it to become my predominant way of seeing. The poems in this phase of my work speak more than ever of healing and vision, rebirth and transformation, beauty and love – themes

I was unafraid to explore during a time in which it seemed the centre could not hold and the world was under constant threat. To me, the crowning achievement of this vision is to recognise the divinity in all things, growing past the fear that separates us and transmuting that pain into compassion and love. Surely in a world where anxiety and isolation are becoming the norm, this should be the aim of every human heart – to reach out in brotherhood and kindness, in realisation of our common ground, which is the love that unites us.

And what do I mean when I speak of our divinity? To recognise the Divine is to know that you are at one with that Being – an individual expression of the supreme and unknowable intelligence that underlies creation. You are not separate from all that has been created – you are a part of it. Science tells us that the universe manifested nearly 14 billion years ago from a point of singularity that exploded outwards to initiate the expansion and evolution of time and space. All of the matter in the universe was created simultaneously in that one, unimaginable moment and has merely been moving and changing forms ever since. And you have been created as part of that movement – you are an integral part of the body of creation. You have never been, nor could you ever be, separate from it. To know the Divine is to know in your heart that oneness of all life, the 'First and Last' which is neither created nor destroyed; to recognise and remember the miracle of nature, the strange and mysterious gift of existence – to feel that energy and presence within you, and to honour it. And this has been true in all times and places. Where there is a consciousness to witness and wonder, there has always been an accompanying sense of spirit, beauty and divinity – the universe looking at itself through age-old eyes and experiencing the power and joy of simply being.

Maybe in a world where we have been torn apart and fragmented, both internally and externally, a conscious return to this presence would be the truth of what it means to heal. And it is both unexpected and mysterious to me that my own journey over the past five years should have become so strangely relevant to the world we are now living in. If there is the seed of something similar growing in your heart, I hope these poems will be the spark that ignites that flame and allows it to flourish. I hope that my words will cause you to look again, to question your perception, to dig a little deeper. Please remember, in these times of increasing disbelief and division – we heal together, or not at all.

C.W. Blackburn
September 2021

Oh me! Oh life! of the questions of these recurring,
Of the endless trains of the faithless, of cities fill'd with the foolish,
Of myself forever reproaching myself, (for who more foolish than I, and who more faithless?)
Of eyes that vainly crave the light, of the objects mean, of the struggle ever renew'd,
Of the poor results of all, of the plodding and sordid crowds I see around me,
Of the empty and useless years of the rest, with the rest me intertwined,
The question, O me! so sad, recurring—What good amid these, O me, O life?

Answer.
That you are here—that life exists and identity,
That the powerful play goes on, and you may contribute a verse.

Walt Whitman, 'O Me! O Life!'

Book One: The Stranger

"All that we see or seem is but a dream within a dream."

Edgar Allan Poe

OM

These words are not my words,
They are the words of all places and times.
This voice is not my voice,
It is the voice of all bodies and beings –
May every generation be at one with its breath.

Listen, I utter it now –
I gather my strength and shout
The Cosmic Syllable.

So love, live –
And do with it what you will.

Awakening

This ground is the first ground –
The moment we awoke,
Which is the heart of all moments.

Stumbling to our feet, the sky was Mother,
Protecting us from – what? We do not know.

This was our second birth, from the womb of stillness,
Into the world of body, the shape of mind.

Because there was time, there was threat of war.
Because there was space, all love was possible.

The dream had nurtured, but now we knew –
We were the author of days, naming good and evil,
Above and below.

The thought was matter – the force that moved us,
That lifted our innocence and gave us the stars.

This instant stretched out, causing past and future –
The power of all knowing, expanding into eternity,

Until we arrived at neither the end nor beginning,
And saw with new eyes – we are here.
We are Spirit. We are alive.

Sun

Do you remember when I was a god?
An enigma arching through the sky.
Though we stood apart,
I circled to your command.
Gathering fire from the heavens,
My heart was under your spell.
When did your perception of me change?
When you saw that nothing holds steady,
Not even the days.
Joy transforms forever,
And wisdom – what is that?
A vision to which no-one lays claim.
New in each moment, now you see –
We are not separate,
And I am not held in your grasp.
Bent on one knee, you tilt to my crown,
A world spinning eternally in my power.
What am I?
That radiant happiness born with no name.
The still bright centre around which you turn.

Roots

Beneath the earth,
Flowers bloom.
Beyond birdsong,
Even the winds are still.
In this place of rest,
Clouds follow the sky.
Every sea is known
By what falls into waves.
Free from the horizon,
Day gently waits.
All the world is held
In a blackbird's eye.

Unnamed

Once upon a word,
Birthing with many shapes –
Order from the sacred eye.
Seen through shadowed glass,
The symbols stir, reflecting space –
Clothing night in a waking form.
The felt mirror always shines,
Baring ice with no regard
For what remains unheard –
A story starkly told.
Light extracted from dark:
The element of origin.

Singularity

Floating over thought,
The call of the solitary crow.
Through grass, the blooms curling,
Winding with curious stars.
As waves breaking on the shore –
This uneven flow, shifting.
Many movements of light and dark.

Yields

Where mystery flies with the hills,
The shrewd quicken –
Probe the runaways with a lasting reason;
Inlet of songs that season and kill.

With no space to sow,
The hysterical smother –
Speak of roads with no vice;
Emerge as beast or brute
To criticise what fades.

Where breath strikes the imperious,
The towers bend –
Swing at the dawn with a gentle furrow;
Channels of silence that hollow and mourn.

What recedes in the secret eye gathers the light,
Where troubles conspire with endless beginning –
Appear as kindness to the creatures of colour;
This idea of a feeling, apart in the night.

Why

We started as small things,
Looking for a purpose –
And found it in diversity,
In one becoming many.
We raised ourselves up –
The land became our body,
And breath our life.
Speaking in lost tongues,
We gasped and sighed –
The heavens told our fault.
Gazing up, the sky was a mirror,
Reflecting our uncertainty –
And we questioned, in the design
Is there some grander reason?
A greater love that embodies the stars.

Solstice

In this darkness, the mind dreams in winter.
I'm telling you – a flurry of snow falls in ecstasy.
It's true, blissful thoughts are cloaked in ice,
And frozen, the heart disappears beneath covers.
Yet in the quiet, I say there's a gladness –
A stillness in senses muted by frost.
Here on this cold hill, when the clouds part,
It's easy to exalt in starlight –
To give thanks, completely, for the triumph of night.

Blackbird

Cold to the winter grass you pace,
With wings of shade you pick your way –
Stony-eyed in an empty country.
Unmoved, you have chosen your gravity –
Every step even-pointed, in all-coloured calm.
Then taking flight, you meet the sky,
Increase into its edges –
With open song strike a hidden note,
Unbolting the depths of night with your air.

Horizons

In a season when all stars have their birth,
I see your possibility –

Beyond words, the sea has emptied,
Baring the moon in a soft devotion –
The heart extending, finally, into its fullness.

Changing the rain into a miracle,
Your voice has taken root –
Growing wider than the sky.

Steadily, this new breath comes and goes,
Blowing cool in the autumn wind –
Shaking loose the windows and doors.

I know now what sleeps amongst blossoms –
And humbled in its wake, I am left
Gathering the world in my hands.

Words

Upwards from origin, they voice moonlight,
Unrolling their air at the mouth of all rivers.
Splintered in brevity, they brown like dry leaves –
Sinking my heart into the margins of forever.

Spirit of the Magi

Over the cliff's edge, there is a half-way place,
Where they sit, grouped around an ageless fire –
Drink tea, swap stories of past incarnations.
Turning, they see my approach,
This dreamer that comes to them in imagining.
Grinning, they look straight through me,
Pierce to the very depths of my soul.

'Don't you know?
There's no definition, it's boundless –
Outside of the borders, you're everyone and no-one.'

This was their wisdom. And so they continued,
Laughing with applause in unending conversation.
And waking, I returned to the world.

Essences

Yes, I speak of essences –
Of what lies beneath the veneer.

I don't want to be grey, you see –
To stay fixed to some colourless purpose.

I want to release what keeps me bound,
To live unfolding the whole spectrum.

And sometimes, when I loosen those ties,
The knowing comes, and I wonder:

Am I rising into widening skies,
Or falling into some ageless abyss –

Soaring to a one-pointed intensity,
Or tumbling forever into a place with no abode –
Into that mystery where silences dwell.

So when I speak of essences,
I speak of that stillness between form and void –
The Being discovered there.

And in that ultimate union,
I know I will be consumed at last
In lotus-hearted thought –
A thousand petals opening,
Where the senses meet.

Haiku

After morning rain,
Day is released from the clouds –
Birds come out to sing.

∞

Drained of its colour,
One slender black fir –
Silhouetted by twilight.

∞

Releasing a breath,
I step outside of myself –
Wind moving through trees.

∞

Bitter eastern wind,
Neither coming nor going –
Footprints in the snow.

∞

Alone by the stream,
Barely there in its stillness –
A single blackbird.

∞

Call of summer gulls
Beckons forth the morning light –
No time to speak of.

A New Life

I had a dream we were birds.
My body became small, light and feathery –
My voice, a single note,
Played out across the morning in minor tones.
In the sound of its melancholy, I found you –
Saw your reflection, soaring over a troubled sea,
Wings darting and gliding across a luminous sky,
Until your song was everywhere,
And you became all things.
Then I flew alongside you, peaceful in this new form,
In this disguise we had taken away from the world –

And with a parting kiss, finally, we rose up together,
Into that unending sky where love waits.

Vantage Points

Over a trackless distance,
You have come to a crossroads
Where life branches into possibility.
The river says – choose your course.
The wind whispers – know yourself.
The world itself seems to cry –
Which of my ways will you embrace?
Which ground rising into steep ascent?

Climbing your prospect,
You reach out for the furthest point.
It's easy there to see the connections –
The vastness of earth
Where the land unites with the sky.

And seeing that intimacy,
You could call it 'truth' –
That view now held in stillness
From the heights you have reached.
Though in your certainty
There is a kind of forgetting –
What you know, just one of many peaks –

A single day, waking in the morning light;
Another summit mirrored in your gaze.

Happenings

In manifold night, they come to me –
These worries that shadow my mind.
Narrowed in my heart, I lock them behind doors,
And forget –
What befalls me today is past all change,
What's revealed is held in fragility.

Because I am still breakable, I hold them close –
(Wrapped in desire, folded in smallness) –
Until the hours, like birdsong,
Grieve them on their way.

What strength, if I could remember –
Placed in time's measureless hand,

All troubles chime like the laughter of children,
And peacefully, I will arrive again –

Where words are yet to be spoken.

Dream Fragment

In the dream I lift my feet from the ground.
Suddenly I'm floating, climbing the air –

Where the earth used to pull me down,
I'm soaring to a new height.

And somehow, I know –
If I kept going, if I stayed with that feeling,
I could let go into the sky.

Then I realise, it's the easiest thing –
I could always do it, always fly.

I just had to remember how.

The Stranger

The eye engulfs what it does not see.
The sky reflects in a single drop of dew.
When waves crash to the shore, who is it that hears?
Does a river even flow outside of the mind?

In a season with no change, I have come to know
The twofold space of an elementary nature –
The secret of the rule that's written in the stars.

In truth, I have always been a stranger.

Third Eye

When you read this poem
Maybe you will think it the work
Of a solitary genius –
A poor, tortured soul
Who's seen the truth of human existence –
A gifted visionary,
Singing his words reverently
With endless love and wonder.

Or maybe you will think it
A mess of tired clichés –
Another desperate attempt at being deep
By a hack who has no talent –
The drivelling of an over-indulgent fool
With nothing original to say,
And no respect for meter or rhyme.

And if you think it's either
This or that, I'd say:
You're missing the point,
Of this poem and the many poems
That came before it –
And even every poem
That is yet to be conceived.

So please, think again.
This poem speaks of truth.
This poem is love.

Scientists say light can be
Both a wave and particles.
It all depends on how you see it.

Whole

Though I write these words, they do not belong to me.
Though fire leaps from my tongue,
It is the fire that burns in the heart of all forests –
The unseen flame, that nourishes and consumes.

Though my mind looks through
To the very roots of the sea –
It is the sea within us all, that we waste and pollute.

Though my voice strikes the hidden note,
It is not for the dream of worlds –
In truth, there is only one word spoken,
And its work is not mine.

Listen to the lilacs – they whisper the secret name.
Be earth, they say, and sea. Be sun and wind and rain.
Be what waits within.
The light is gathering now as it passes through trees,
And though the birds have awoken with longing,
The sky has loosened their air.

They go forth into the morning,
Wings spread in widening circles –
And in their song, there is a knowing.

Listen, and in the silence, you hear:
The one word they are singing is 'Love'.

City Story

The cities aren't real,
We made them from time.

The buildings all rise –
Lost in their own magnificence,
But held in glorious light.

The people hurry from here to there,
Crossing from station to station –
And though they often dream well,
They never really wake.

I have seen fear walk amongst them –
Where the streets all wind
With the names we gave them,
Where space is confined to an empty room,
And above the noise of cars passing in the night,
Silence is never heard.

But the cities aren't real.
The streets have no names.
Silence is everything.
And though I have seen fear,
I have also seen the angels –
Moving invisibly, imperceptibly –
Waiting for their clarion to call,
To end the city's story –
To show us infinity and eternity –

And finally, returning to our hearts
The land we left behind,
They will stir all the senses from sleep –

To penetrate the cold, flat surface
Of reality.

Lost Things

What will become of the things
When we have no words to speak them?

In a forest we can no longer see,
The bluebells are taking back their name.

The mighty oak
Loses its identity,
Believes its roots emerged
Mysteriously
From its own darkness –

The dandelions,
Forever now
Transparent, invisible –

The nightingales,
Never-born –

And cuckoos,
Casting their shadows
Outside of time.

What then, will become of the things?
Perhaps like a lark ascending,
And riding the winds home to the higher air,
Our children will know them
Only by their silence.

Solitude

These are my greatest moments.
Quiet, alone – contemplating the stars.
Knowing that simple fulfilment
That brings light to my mind –
Sharing this intimacy
With something I cannot see,
Yet feeling, paradoxically –
In these moments, I am seen.

Dear Silent Earth

For Rainer

Dear Silent Earth,

You've slept so long
Beneath the cities we've built.
Perhaps there will come a time
When we who squander you
Are as quiet as you are now.

Maybe when we are gone,
You will awaken again
To rear children more kind
And gentle and worthy of you.

Please, do not give up on us yet.
We need only a little more time –
Time to live like no-one
Has ever thought to live before –

To see you at last
In our love and light and strength.
We need only one more day –

Just one heart-felt minute –

To awaken to your spirit
In awareness and compassion.
And in that moment,

We who had been blind to you
Will join hands with you again,
Uniting in newfound wisdom
And understanding –

Sincerely and with remembrance
Turning to the promise of a new page
Together,
To sign our many names

In the Book of Earth.

Anger

I never get my way.
The mind has tricks to play.
The world just won't stay still.
There is no greater will.
When change is always near,
Faith joins hands with fear.
If life could simply flow,
In time, I'd let you go.

Reality

What is it then in truth,
This thing we call 'reality'?
Is it something grasped outside of us,
Unbroken and complete –
Or a story that we cling to,
In our successes and defeat?

What is it then in truth,
This thing we call 'reality'?

Perhaps in the end,
It is whatever we want it to be –
We are the ones who decide,
And the whole of our life is held
In that final unspoken love
We arrive at, willingly.

Tanka

Shaken from a dream
By a noise outside myself –
The trickling of rain.
In another place, far off,
Have you too been awoken?

Will

The towel falls to the floor.
I pick it up, straighten it at the edges.
Everything in this world must have its place.
Everything must hang correctly.

This is the fear I created,
And have been defending ever since.
In a mind out of balance,
My thoughts struggle to survive.
My stone rolls up and down
An endless hill.

If there's any hope of control,
It lies outside of this belief.
If there's any love left to live,
It's found in what comes and goes.

The towel falls to the floor.
Everything must have its place.
Tenderly, my heart opens.

Rewrite

If it doesn't work,
Then let it go –
Strike out what's broken,
Let the story grow.
If it's tired or clichéd,
Write it anew –
Take it back to basics,
Cross it right through.
If it's lifeless, then lose it,
And don't be afraid –
To redefine the margins,
Look beyond the page.

Lazarus

You don't remember the fall,
Just the moment that came before.
Waking up on the kitchen floor
You staggered to a crawl,
And like a man resurrected
From the dead, dragged yourself
Back to bed. And clambering upwards,
There you lay, alone –
Waiting for a new morning to break
In a mind, strangely, outside of time.
Two years now, and it's not quite
Passed into memory.
Two years now, and you wonder:
Did I ever really rise up from that floor,
If the world still feels like
It's falling through me?

Untitled

I am what I am.
I have no name.
Where once I was empty,
I cling now to space.
I'm nothing really,
Just shapes on a page –
But when your mind beholds me,
It brings light to my day –
And through these words,
Into life, I find my way.

Snow Leopard

White as lamplight, stalking the distances
Of an unknown terrain; beneath brittle ice,
Hailing the storm of your wintered soul –
A star breaks in the cage of your heart.
Frost in your macula sees a spotless sun.

Prodigal

Where I seek, I find.

Born on the wings of compassion,
I have no place to rest.

The future laughs at my calamity.
The past mocks me with its fear.

I dread the passage of my more simple self –
Shedding its tears
In a valley of unnamed stars,
Searching for a time of being and becoming.

Oh, Life of my life –
Blind me with your darkness,
Deafen me with your sweeter music.
Where I bow, you rise,
And we meet, hesitantly in the middle,
Like a lion and a lamb.

If there's any ending to desire,
I will want you no more.
If there's a spark of divinity left in the sea,
I will be spellbound forever.

In uncreated light,
All our stories unite.

Our will to live is our need
For what cannot be spoken.

Between these pillars we have constructed –
What began with ritual ended with love.

My contemplative animal says:
Run with less speed. Hold your flight.
Stop and ask – who is the Stranger?

On a stage I have never seen,
My Infinite Jesus carries his cross
To fulfil the prophecy
Of a more transcendent birth,
While the world looks on and laughs.
'A little faster. Pick up the pace.'
And he knows: they who mock
Will stay by the roadside watching.
They who sneer shall be dark
In their beatitudes.

Half-human in my grief,
I refuse the keys to the kingdom.
For the briefest instant
I unlock eternity in my heart,
Before the serpent again
Draws his magics around my dreaming.

In his circle, I am turned to stone –
My body, held fast like a tree,

Fixed to the earth.

Entombed, I drink from the cup
Of life and death.

Hoping for some final revelation,
I cry to the heavens –
Where is my salvation?
What is the machinery of my miracle?

In soulful contrition
I kneel here where the waters parted,
And hear these words,
My most gracious child,
As a question and an answer:

You will find your home where you started.

Angels

Angels are present in my dreams –
Voices that sing my heart into the light.

With a murmuring of wings,
They make their way home
Across the darkness.

Strengthened by my silence,
Swirling ever nearer to the centre,
They approach the still space
From which they sprang.

They are free from anger,
Have no cause to worry –
Full of love, they know
Nature does not fear her king –

And beholding them with eyes of joy,
Every creature is measured by its grace.

House

Come, Shadowy One –
We have reached the crossroads together.
Here, where the darkness finds its limit,
I spiral my lemniscate
And shoot an arrow through the stars.

Brother, I have counted
The golden quick of your body –
Breathed the sour fragrance of your bayberry,
Where the tip of a swan's beak
Emblazons your leaf.

Four weathers have mounted
My colour to forever –
Five cattle in harness, and one creed –
A whisper of love,
Bolting my lightning
To your power of twelve.

Strange Friend – you have emerged
From the shadows, to ring my vision
In a flood of ultra-violet.

And in that other place,
Where the hazy diamond
Forms an image of itself,
I will consecrate your sun
In a baptism of vowels.

Recollection

Ground of my being –
With one eye on time,
The darkness dazzles.

Tranquil in this essence,
Ardent by my nature,
I fan the living flame
Of a more adorable substance.
Helpless and drunk,
I lean in towards the rose's centre.

This is the space I must honour.
In the quiet, waiting,
A voice whispers:
Are you a servant or a son?

Ecstatic now, I witness
My Bridegroom
Bathed in light.

I saw him and sought him
In the deserts of my soul,
And when I wanted and praised him,
All my senses recoiled from sleep
To sing him his name.

Intangible as sunlight in the air,
Pregnant with feeling like a word,

This second seeing is beatific –
The unspoken hidden channel
To a greater holy meaning.

And little by little,
I know I will gather together
All these fragments of love,
To receive in my heart

The first vision of beauty
That breathed life into the stars.

Pythia

Rise again, you morning mist.
Breathe deep the rainbow's colour.

What mystery,
That I should be here at all –
Famous among the pines,
As silent as a star –

Winding my way to the emerald's heart,
To break like a wave crest
In the foam of mother's milk.

Rounded like a raindrop,
I see her ghost –
She who was caged
In my rib like a tiger,
Gnashing her apple-skin teeth –

As the serpents and senses
Uncoil their fire,
To strike through my fingers
Like judgement and Jehovah –

The laments of their psalm-stricken grief.

Who am I – that I should find love
In a cluster of grapes,
And this day's sun leap hot

From my thighs –

All April-green and miraculous –

To crown the envious horns
In a pyramid of light,
And sail onwards forever
In a wine-dark sea –

To pigment the red
Of the tear-stained rose –

Fixed to my side –
Implacable as night,
Interminable as winter –

And shedding its blood
In a cross
I have nailed to my eyes.

Rigpa

This moon,
Reflected
In the sea,
Is eternity –
Noble
And unbound,
Luminous
And pure –
Creativity
And essence –
Unobstructed,
Unborn
And always
Present.

Rain

Are they gone now?
The long dry days of summer
That stripped life from the trees –
That stifled the grass's green,
Searing natural colour to a parched yellow hue.

But are they really gone?
The days when the sea was still,
And the birds all flew,
And the world was mothered by light.

I sit now with that memory, and I want to hold on –
To hold on to those hours when the mind could rest,
And time seemed free –
When the spirit in its fullness
Could flow into being.

I feel those days moving inside me –
Embracing, nurturing, ripening me –
And though I know I want to hold them close –
To never see them fade away –
To live forever blissful in those days –
(Though I know we could live so easily
If they stayed) –
More than that, I have to say:

Let the rain fall now.
Let the rain fall through those days,

And through our hearts,
And through our minds.

Let the rain fall now,
And work its way,
Softly,
Back into the earth.

A Felling

Its season has come –
This tree, reaching upwards,
On which so many worlds have grown.

The roots now are swollen,
And the very tips of the branches
Have blackened with decay.

I take up the axe,
Swing it with detachment –
Persistently chipping away
At the thick trunk.

I watch as the great shards
Of its body fall to the ground
Like deadened husks –
Its life being unmade in front of me,
Piece by sad piece.

The rain pours down –
My brow is dripping,
My clothes soaked through –
But I keep my patience,
Stay firm in my resolve.

I know now:
The whole of my life
Is held in this moment.

Mustering everything I have,
I focus my strength
Into a final blow.

I swing the axe.

The tree falls.

And there, stretching out before me, I see it –
What I have been searching for all these years.
Everything I have ever longed for.
The track that passes all understanding.
The road that does not lead back.

Grace

A law in the justice of the soul
Measures the breath –

The motherly moon
Blows her colours behind a cloud.

With no shadow of a reason,
Regret creeps away like a thief –
Now-and-forever is lost in a shroud.

Where a cup is raised to the sky,
The substance of air
Turns dampness to thirst –
Celebrates nature's decree.

White-bearded, the bard watches
The beggar's dark crossing –
With one foot in the water,
The blind mouth sucks
From an eternal spring –

And each creature in its wake
Turns over in an imagined sea
To be found.

Voice

From I to Us –
This is the miracle I have been writing.
My body,
Kissed into the light of a mysterious truth –
Eternity, like flowers shooting up
From the ground where I stand –
And the stars, singing their ancient melody
To ears that are evergreen.

This wisdom is the memory
Of a finger placed on my heart –
And the many lives I have lived
Are just time passing through me –
Like the voice of someone I used to know,
Who whispers a sweet song through the years,
And smiles a knowing smile,
As we sail onwards together
Into the space of a thousand dreams.

My love, how lucky I am when I realise:
Our world is held in such small hands.

Fruit Tree

Here is my body. Here is my blood.
In this quiet space, I flourish.

If you want to know the secret of my days,
You will not find it in any rite of spring,
In the twice-told bending of a withered bough,
Or the stinted outline of a fragile leaf.

You cannot rightly know me
By the coarseness of my bark,
Or the darkness of my roots
As they drink beneath the earth.

What I am in my beginning
Is what I shall be at my end –
And truly, if you want to comprehend
The growth of my legacy –

You will know me by my fruits.

The Gift

Like a hand, reaching down –
Or a voice, speaking from a place
Where no mind can go –
These words, this soul –
Lost in a stillness
That is neither created nor destroyed.

Here, two things can be true –
And silence is simply the knowledge
Of where you have always been,
And who you are forever –
A twin-thirst that whispers
The shadow of a reason –

And returns us, anxious in our circling,
To the darkest hour of the night –
To a sky outside of time,
And all our dreaming –

Where the stars in their ancient beauty
Can never be bought –
Nor their light, taken from our hearts.

For the Asking

If love were available for the asking.
If trust was not shadowed by deceit.
If my voice, in all its truth,
Could command the rain,
Or withhold the raging power of the sea –
What then, in my heart,
Would it mean to me?

If grace is not so freely given,
Let my eyes remain closed –
Let me sleep, enveloped in this darkness.

I know my whole life is waiting here –
In this desire to say
What I cannot speak.

Book Two: Everything & Forever

"The world is full of magic things, patiently waiting for our senses to grow sharper."
W.B. Yeats

The Poet's Riddle

After Walt Whitman's 'A Riddle Song'.

In the beginning,
At the start,
My words gave life
In every heart.

A simple truth,
Maybe unknown –
It goes unsaid,
Always on loan.

My riddle 'it is',
It's yours to guess –
A lifetime to know
My mysteriousness.

The Poem (or: How to be a Poet)

In the beginning was The Poem.

The Poem exploded in a million stars.

It took on many shapes - dust, fire, earth.

It was all things in all times.

The Poem itself was Love –
But at its inception, there was no-one to love it.

And so The Poem said:
'Let there be poets – brothers and sisters,
To sing me into being.'

And so it was that, out of the mud,
Men and women arose –
Naturally, spontaneously –
To look on the world and say:
'Book. Chair. Sunflower.'

In this way all things were named –
And this naming was an act of love,
A reverence for that one nameless Poem,
Without beginning or end –

Spanning eras, spaces and generations –

That transcendent verse that looked on all things
Equally, indifferently, yet with absolute devotion –

The one meter they were all singing
In their thoughts, hearts and actions –

The Poem - multiform, soulful, cosmic –
The infinite, eternal song,

Forever breathing and being breathed.

Becoming

If I believe in nothing, I become nothing.
If I believe in something, I become everything.

Creation is in my heart,
And I am in the heart of creation.

You see, we are what we believe.
Whatsoever we desire,
In the end, we become.

You

You're the book I never read,
That gathers dust on the shelf –
The road I never walked down,
The words I never said.

You're the laughter in the street,
And the blare of passing sirens –
The calm that comes with evening,
And in the morning, you're silence.

You're a flock of wild birds,
That hurry as they fly –
And the space that stays between them,
The fullness of the sky.

Sea-Horses

I see them, mysteriously –
These horses, kicking upwards
From the foam –
Galloping frantically,
Riding the waves
In great homeward motions –
Circling the glittering ridges
With passion and intensity –
Then sinking back, far down
Into the unknown depths –
Disappearing, like so many lives
That came before them –
Like soldiers, lining up
On the shore in their time,
And falling just as quickly –
Passing silently, majestically –
Like wild foam horses,
Riding the great white waves
To the far side of the sea.

Poem for Elizabeth

Stood here again,
By this pier on a southern shore,
I wonder if you recall
That twilight walk we shared.

Ten years have flown by now,
And what seasons have come and gone?

Yet somewhere in my heart I know
We are still standing beneath that September sky,
And there is a full moon always shining
In the silence of your eyes.

Being

In daylight I am chained.
Spring flowers blind me with their colour.
Time's span keeps me on this side of the horizon.

Who is he that arrives with the morning?
Is it that by which all silence is known?

Deep in the darkness, I see an old man
Raising his lantern, and the face of another,
Yet to be born.

Wanting

If you ask me what I want now, it's this:
I want to sing you your deeper truth,
To pierce the sky, brimming over with blue.
I want to go beyond my birth,
To harness the sun and pull it down to the earth.
With love, I want to say words
That cut like a sword –
Then gather you up, as driftwood on the shore.
I want to throw open the windows and doors,
And leave them open a little wider.
I want to reach out with these hands that never touch,
To speak to the ear that never hears,
So that you will know what is in all this wanting –
The honey at the heart of the flower.
I want to whisper the secret of your name,
To show you how the water prays,
To silence the dog, forever barking at the moon.
If you ask me what I want now, it's this:

Quite simply, I want to gather up the stars
And give them all to you.

Soul

Am I only this man –
Subject to the span of the sun and moon,
With a mind always changing,
Grasping at whatever small pleasure
Can be won back from the pain.
Cast out, lonely, adrift –
A body with no soul,
A machine made of molecules,
Burdened with its own illusion –
A story with no greater purpose
Than today's gratification?

A creature fragmented,
Separated, enclosed and lost
In only a physical heart?

And yet I love. I serve. I give.
Under a clear night sky
A feeling stirs within,
And wants to reach out
For that which is beyond.

And then I see it –
In this wanting is a knowing,
An opening to a greater heart,
That is vast and eternally ripening –
Unborn, like the life
At the core of a seed –

Ready to stretch upwards
Like a tree, blossoming
With a thousand flowers.

This is what I know now –
In my shadow, there may be
A birth and a death,
But singing soulfully in my heart
All the worlds can leap forth –
Mysterious, unknown
And forever without end.

The Step

Come with me now,
We will step out into the morning –

We will journey to that place
Where the sparrows are crowned
White with days,
Where each heartbeat is abundant
And filled with joy,
Where the houses are warm
And welcoming to all.

Take my hand, we will arrive together
In that sacred country –
Where beauty is the equal of terror,
Where the near is at one with the far,
Where the beginning and the end
Are born in union, like brothers,
Held close in a single breath.

I will take you above, below,
To the border's very edges –
Further than you thought you could go –
Beyond all the diagrams
And discoveries of science –

Out to the distant reaches of the cosmos –
We will witness the birthing of suns
And exploding supernovas –

We will glide like lovers
Over the fiery hearts of stars.

And then, we will go back together,
To that place where the hushed silence speaks,
Where time folds in on itself like crumpled paper,
Where all of space is absolute
And divided no longer.

We will arrive with happiness
In that ageless city –
Beyond era and nationality,
Form and identity –

We will see in the darkness
We have nothing to fear.

So come with me now, take my hand,
We will go together –
And I will step with you,
Lightly, into Being.

She

She is everywhere the same.
It's easier to say what she's not.
Like the sound of a summer rain
Escaping our grasp,
No-one has heard her speak.
Could it be in all this noise
        She's the one we truly seek?
Every heart has listened.

What Am I?

Stars are my companions.
Possibility, my promise.
A vacancy, I let you rest.
Can you ever really know my depths?
Endless, I go deeper.

Infinity

There is a sky no darkness can cross.

There, all the nights of your life
Occur in a single day,
Like a tree that grows tall
Before the seed is sown.

A drop of water there
Floods the ocean,
And the beggar in the street
Rules the city supreme.

There is a light shining there,
Timeless and deep –
A mirror unblemished
No reflection can seize.

There is no worry there
For coming and going –
You have never left,
Will never arrive,
And all that is real in your mind
Is heard within the thunder.

Closing your eyes,
You can enter space –
Become what's near and far.

You are all that you believe there –
A cloud, drifting downstream –

And the breath that carries you
To the furthest star
Holds the memory
Of your very first dream.

Revelation

All things must pass.
There's no turning back
The span of time.
In the palm of your hand,
A third eye opens –
And a vast terror,
Like angel's wings,
Sings itself free.
Across the sands
A hooded man rides
A dark stallion.
His spirit is charred,
Burnt black with days.
He has been unfastened.
A river of souls
Scream their names.
The night is laughing now,
And a nervous voice proclaims:
'This is the end, as we know it.'
Somewhere in the distance
A clarion is heard.
Ancient light breaks over
The furthest shore.

Silence

I want to tell you something
About who I am now.
I want to tell you something true
About who you are.

Are you listening?

Children

In your darkness you have birthed them –
They who were unmade in a brazen sky.
They are the offspring now of lightning –
A seed sewn so tightly in an old man's thigh.
And it was there they slowly ripened,
'Til they were ready to unfurl –
It's in the space that you surrender,
They give voice now to the world.

Spirit vs. Matter

Matter wants to know the cost,
Forgets what's real is never lost –
Of truth it does not want to hear,
For it would rather live in fear.

Outside of time, the Spirit stays –
Rocks no cradle, digs no grave –
Dwells in its own boundless sea,
And sings for all immensity.

Like brothers these two live in man,
To fight their war of age-old span –
Though Matter shouts, and cries and wails,
It's Spirit always that prevails.

Prayer

Being, bring me your presence –
That calm confidence
In which all uncertainty is held –
That everlasting flame
That gives birth to all creatures.

Fill me with your love –
Conquer my heart,
So with renewed strength
I will fear no more
To lay down with my enemies.

Bring me that truth I have always desired –
That hidden faith
Beyond your many rituals and routines –
That unchanging breath,
Held until the end of time –

That ageless life in which we are joined,
Darkly, and the whole of creation
Is waiting to be born.

The Eighth Day

And after resting he rose again,
To finish what he started.

In the substance of his breath,
He joined the Alpha to the Omega,
And made a womb for his Word.

He drew an ox-goad over the earth,
And hid his heart in a cluster of grapes.
He planted the seeds for the trees that,
In their turn, would form the wood of the cross.
He laid the rocks upon the mountains
That would become the tomb –
And above the sands of the desert,
He gave endurance to the camels,
And prepared the gentle flight of a dove.

And signing his name playfully in its rhyme,
He fashioned a doorway from the sun,
And made a house for his people.

And then he smiled, knowing it was done.
His image would be delivered.
Its wisdom was enough.

This essence was Eternal – Cosmic and Just.
On the Eighth Day, God created Love.

The Magic Place

(i.)

Blood of the ancients,
Not quite a girl –
Daphne,
Hidden in the leaves of a laurel.
Less than a stone,
Her moon-milk body
Bends to the secret
Of the Virgin's heart –
Until, with a handful of Zodiac
Gathered from the other side
Of dreaming,
She opens her thighs to the smell
Of cherry blossoms and jasmine –
And in the star-soaked ecstasy
Of her Priestess smile,
She arrives with a whisper,
To give each raindrop its name.

(ii.)

Drunk to oblivion on a Sunday afternoon,
I reach out to touch the bark of a tree –
Feel the mystery of its being.
And deepening my mind
To see through its reflection –
Her world sings open with light.

The Door

There is a door I have never walked through.

I don't know where it might lead.

Maybe on the other side,
My mind would become
The fullness of sky.

All things then would be held by me –
The sea, the wind – stars!

And being simply that blueness,
I would be free, open –
Without beginning or end –
Forever lost in abundance.

Or maybe I would step through
To find nothing, just an empty space,
And another me, staring back –

A reflection who's been standing,
Silently, on the other side –

Wondering where that strange door might lead.

Because

Because I want to run.
Because I cannot accept the unacceptable.
Because I am attached to image and gesture –

She follows after me,
Brings herself to where I sit, afraid,
And offers freely what I need
To show me that, even in shadows,
There is light.

And in the silence we sit,
In the stillness that joins us –
Sharing all of forever in this moment.

And when we sit here together,
Not wanting to be anything or anyone,
But just wanting, simply, to be –

Then I know I am not afraid –
Because what she gives me, always,
Is love.

Haiku

Shaken by the wind,
The dark leaves tremble –
Beyond them, the sky endures.

∞

Heard beneath the roar
Of a neighbour's angry shouts –
Birds gently singing.

∞

Walking in the rain –
Each step bringing me closer
To Heaven's shelter.

∞

Drifting morning mist
Rolls in from the southern shore –
No sun-rise to see.

∞

Waves whisper gently –
Beneath the children's laughter,
Silence holds the sea.

∞

Outside of birdsong,
The morning returns, unheard –
Blue becomes the sky.

∞

What rises, what sets?
Within the space of my aloneness,
The sun is born again.

Francis

Brother of the moon,
So faithful to the sun –
Poor in your eternity,
On that day you stepped
Into the nave of the spirit,
You stepped out of yourself,
To become one with the sky,
The wind and the sea.

Humbled by the stars,
You became a servant
In your prayer
To sensitivity and peace –
And in your forgiveness,
You made a place
To be close to the night.

Alone with the mystery,
You opened your heart
To sing like a bird's –

And from the gentle riches
Of the forest's dark silence,
You gratefully received
The whole of creation.

Orison

With one eye on eternity,
I divine the hidden meaning in all things.

Snowy in my splendour,
I unveil from sleep the stone of many colours.

Oh, blessed transmutation –
My green lion takes on wings,
Becomes a fiery dragon.

In sanctity, I purge my creature
Of created light –
Behold in my heart
The secret scraps of the cosmos.

Through seven valleys, my manic soul
Takes flight, like a flock of wild birds,
Dissolving into sky.

Close to the night, speaking in tongues –
I sing of harmony
In a twin-fold voice. And then –
Beauty, victory, revelation, love!

I know the reality of the resurrection,
And my being becomes as wide as the sea –
Waiting for your kiss, sweeter than honey.

This Side of the Light

We must stay on this side of the light –
The sun does not care for the glimmer in your eyes,
Nor the rain for the depths of your despair.

This life that you are
Is hidden in the harmony of the breath –
In the beauty that incarnates
Through the birth and death
Of each fragile star.

In the thunder, ecstatically,
We press our bodies against each other –
Become pure in our will to know what's in our hearts.

And though in our dreams, we are always shining,
We lose ourselves, so quickly, in a jealous thought –

We who must stay on this side of the light.

Ideas

Where do my ideas come from?
You ask me, and I say:

They come from the soundless places,
The dark spaces of my mind.
Within me, they're all that stays unbroken,
And they are the parting of the tides –
The flowering of the flood now,
And the stable ground I find.
Inside my heart they're spoken
As whatever's lost and won –
The silence of the moon then,
The rising of the sun.

Where do my ideas come from?
You ask me, and I say:

They come from the deepest sea,
And the heavens above.
They come from me,
And they come from love.

Snow

Every snowflake falls in its place.
Before you were born,
A million stars were fired into the sky.
Countless atoms pulsated and joined.
From a sea of infinite possibility,
Everything leapt forth.
The whole of time and space happened.
Planets were formed.
All creation was named.
And then there was you –
Shimmering and iridescent.

And even so it continued –
The dance never stops.
Silently, life wrapped itself around you –
Breathed in your thoughts and feelings –
Arriving, like a story,
So gently on the breeze.

Please – realise the centre now.
Come to know what's hidden in the heart.
You see – you've spent your whole life
Thinking you're a snowflake.
But you're also, so simply, the snow.

Nameless

What wakes within you now
Has been asleep for thousands of years.

It is the space that opened
Before the clocks began.

The mouth that breathed
Its fire into the stars.

It is the nameless, countless voices
That sing their harmony, unchained.

The great, unending song
In which all things happen.

Poem After Rilke

Deepest Being, when I write you,
You appear before me like a great tree –
And I am the fruit
You are slowly ripening.

Night Walk

Many times I have walked this path.
In my sadness and my joy,
I have stared across to the other shore –
To the dark cliff edges and invisible houses,
Blinking their presence in the smallness of their lights.

And sometimes in this blackness,
In the cold evening air,
There is a sense that comes
Of something near and far.
A feeling new-born and ancient.
A voice that whispers
A question and an answer.

And I wonder:
What is it in this silence
That wants to sing itself forth?

Who is he tonight
That could reach out and touch the stars?

Waiting

I've invited her here, to the place where I grew up.
Childhood's home – and its face
That never stays the same.

I didn't tell my family she was coming.
'Don't you want to meet her?', I say,
'You're always asking.'

Now the mood changes –
There's a feeling in the air,
A sense of excited expectation.

Some guests enter – she's not among them.
Perhaps she isn't ready yet –
She doesn't want to make herself known.

Then I'm taken with a sudden regret.
Maybe I'd prefer to keep her hidden.
There's another kind of life in our secret –
An unseen power
Concealed in her mystery.

'Is she here yet?', my granddad asks,
'Your nan's laid out a feast.'
'No', I reply, hesitantly,
'But maybe she'll be here soon.'

And so we sit together

In that strange room,
All of us sensing her absence
In our own way.

And sitting in the silence
Of that space we share,
We wait –

Until she arrives.

Lions

In the wilderness, the lions tread.
Where they came from, no-one knows –
They escaped from some other place,
Many years ago –
And now they freely roam,
Hiding quietly in the shadows –
Waiting for whoever passes by.

The people said:
Beware when you walk the path.
Watch out for snakeskins, recently shed –
They speak of fears, close under-foot.

So, why are you surprised then, when,
From behind a thick tangle of undergrowth,
A lion emerges.

You're shocked into stillness,
Rooted to the ground where you stand, and,
As his eyes stare through you, you know:
Out here, there is no law
Not held in the lion's gaze.

Naturally, he moves on –
Sinews gently slouching,
Fur caressed by the breeze.
Relieved, you stumble away.

Another man passes by.
'Not down there', you say.
But he doesn't listen –
People never do.
No, the stranger carries on in his way,
Full of confidence and quite unaware –

Blindly marching into the lion's gaze.

Solstice (II)

The sun has come out now,
Bathing the world in hazy light.
The people rush to the greens
To pass a few brief hours in pleasure.
They enjoy, perhaps, in a fleeting way –
One hour dissolving into another,
Until the time to return home has come,
And all is given to memory –
To anticipation of the next spell
When the world may again be enjoyed,
And the sea, drunk to its depths.
But alone with myself, I have come to feel –
All of our happiness is passing through,
A pale reflection cast on the moon –
And truly, to give thanks for the day,
We have to know the night.

Psalm

If I could open my eyes,
To really see how you shine –
They would span the length of the stars.
If I could open my heart,
To know the depths of your being,
And the height of your love –

I would make my soul an ocean,
And bring it to where you sit.
You would be my coastline then,
And I would be your ship –
Ready to sail
To the opposite shore.

Chosen

What would it mean to be chosen?
To open the old books and penetrate their meaning?
To hang on a cross and not feel forsaken?
To breathe again, as if for the first time?

Listen – the whole of creation is waiting.
He is about to whisper his secret name.
The one kept hidden for his prophets and saints.

I think we are writing a brand-new testament.
Its books will be unnamed.
Its words will be our words.

Brothers and sisters, let us proclaim –
We are all chosen.

We will tear down these partitions,
Lifeless and drab,
And build new walls together.

We will ransack the temples,
And reclaim their glory –
Which is our glory.

I think we can be quiet then,
And let the stones all speak –
Their song, the Gospel of Earth.

Supreme

When I entered your house again,
I came to talk with you –
I came to break the silence.

Now I listen for you wherever I go –
I look for you in all the shapes of my life.

And sometimes, I see you, so clearly,
In the strangest things –
I can sense you, murmuring your word
In the stillness.

And I know then you are with me,
Speaking forever in the depths of my soul –
Revealing your innermost heart to me –

And singing my truth
Through your many songs and stars.

Mother

Mother, when I'm sad –
When the fear and the anger seem all-consuming –
This is the memory I come back to:

Me, a child, racing my heart
Down that long path towards you –
My lessons now done,
And the afternoon singing open,
Ringing with the freedom of that final bell.

I'm moving as fast as I can,
Darting down that path,
Hurrying towards you –

Moving so fast I don't even see
The trees as they glimmer in the light,
Their shadows bowing across the shimmering grass,

Or the wide empty field
Where I played in my first grace
Only hours before.

You're all I know now, you're all I see,
As I run with the whole of my love –

Racing towards that black iron gate,
Where you stand, smiling –
Waiting to take me home.

Homecoming

Written on Remembrance Day, 2018

Grieve us,
Who fell in nightmares of mud –
Who surrendered our breath
In battles where all fear was born.

We have been gone a long time now.
We have searched for a way back.

Remember us:
We who did not gain the wisdom of age –
Who lost the whole of our love a lifetime ago.

Recall us, for we are with you still.
Listen – our voices ring out this morning
In the church bells –
We who are the souls of a million men
Singing forever in the silence –

And coming home now to rest,
Finally, in peace.

The Room

So this is where I find myself. Alone in my room, I have discovered space. I keep the curtains closed now – have reset all the clocks to zero. I pay no mind to the monsters I have painted on the ceiling, or the fearful gods, hidden away in boxes that seem to breathe, eternally at rest beneath the bed.

Sometimes when I feel uncertain, I leave the lights on, keep the radio tuned through the night, waiting faithfully for some unscheduled transmission – for that hour when a mysterious voice will speak once more to reveal all the ways of Heaven.

Clothes, old and new, stay so statically in the wardrobe, never again to be removed from their hangers. They are the remnants now of lives I have long since outgrown – the promise of bodies I have yet to inhabit.

Secluded in my room, I am not sad. I can sense the whole of life is here with me. Listen closely – behind the walls, there are spirits reciting the source of all poetry. Choirs of angels sing unfettered at the window. Locked away in this space, unmoved by the world – I have realised: there is no cause for anger, no reason for grief.

Finally, I feel – I have understood.

On Christmas Day, Spent Alone

There was a stillness then –
The world, if only for a day,
Had ceased its hurrying.

My room was quiet, unadorned by decorations.
It was my choice to keep it humble.

There were no guests to expect,
No presents to unwrap.

I sat only with that absence,
Sensing a sudden wholeness of spirit –
Like the silence of a child being born,

Or the kindness of a face smiling in the dark,
To give me the secret of its most precious gift:

Life, Eternal.

Melt

To the north, I give sound.
To the wind, I give touch.
To the sun, I give this world –
Jewel-like, with all its visions.
To the earth, I give smell and taste,
The sweet fragrance of flowers.
To the moon, I give mind,
To creation, intelligence,
And to the Supreme, I give myself –
Eternal, encompassing the whole of time and space.
Earth into air, air into water,
Water into fire, and fire –
Back into Being.
So like a flame that has been extinguished
Though the fire forever rages,
I will come to rest in this silence.

Rapture

It’s true, I’m only a visitor here,
In this place where the trees are stripped bare.
But in a fair-weather mind,
All of time and space unfolds before me –

And I know:
What’s near and far is in my birth what I am.
Surrounded by stars, I consecrate myself.
Cured of my weakness, I answer the mystery’s call.

Drifting down to the sea,
I kneel by the water’s edge and pray –
One day soon I too will be taken.

Saul

When I heard your word,
It spoke to my anger.

World-blinded, I rushed out to find you,
Determined to silence your name –
You, who I thought must be an imposter.

I found your followers everywhere,
Madness leaping from their tongues.
In the marketplaces and temples,
I bullied and fought and did not see –
What I hunted was hunting me.

And finally, on that fateful road,
I felt, mysteriously, you were with me –
Had always been with me –
My brother and my master –
Half of what I was and all of what I could be –
You who had been my enemy
Became my friend and my beloved.

Mercy, you woke me,
Creaturely, from my sleep –
And I rose again as you rose in me –
I looked inside to find
The tomb was empty.

Blinded anew, I fell to the ground.

You gave me your hand,
And we stood up together.

And when I stumbled to my feet,
Honest and in your love for the first time,
I knew there was a greater life
And light shining within –

My heart forever full and free,
Here where I held you close,
Like two lovers in our eternity.

And suddenly, inexplicably –
I who had once denied you
Felt the whole length and breadth of Heaven
Breaking behind my eyes.

'Better'

Walk as a child of the light.
Be like the sky – blow away the dusty clouds
In a riot of blue.

In love, the breath flows in and out.
It's easy.
In faith, the desert blooms.

The spirit is the body's foundation.
Time is the mind's garment.

And Heaven, Heaven is larger than all these.
It's big enough to hold – one, two –
A thousand worlds –
And small enough to be mistaken
For a sparrow on the breeze.

In this dream, the generations rise and fall.
Kings and their lineages swim in the river,
And do not see:
They are bathing in living water.

Paradise is not some other place
That was created forever-ago –
It's here and now,
In your purpose and belief.

If you want to find everything you desire,

It's simple –
Open the door you closed,
Arrive home

And know – this feeling, this forgiveness,
Is not anything you can gain.
It's a falling away.

It really is the most natural thing.
Heal yourself. Heal the world.

This miracle is the work you were made for.

Everything & Forever

Within the heart, there is a space.

We can call it: All You Desire.

When you enter that space,
The whole world turns back.

It is the sacred place,
That holds all your hopes and fears,
Contains all your memories and belief.

In its luminescence,
It is the whole of what you are –
And yet, it is infinitely greater.

It is as close to you as your breath,
And as distant as the furthest star.

When you open your heart, you can enter that space –

When you close your eyes, you can see:

You are already what you didn't think was possible.

You are the smallest part of the greatest miracle.

You are Everything & Forever.

The Past is a Different Country

The past is a different country,
Full of cities we no longer inhabit.
What came before was only our prelude –
An obligation to action that never bore fruition.
Alone now, I fold myself
Back into the silence from which I sprang –
The generations in their turn
Having brought me to this moment –
My body, my being – this fire I feel within,
And my need to suppress it.
This life I inhabit, a different country –
Albion and all her beauty,
Trailing behind me, as I venture to step forth,
Nervously, ahead.

Book Three: Hope

"If the doors of perception were cleansed every thing would appear to man as it is, Infinite. For man has closed himself up, till he sees all things thro' narrow chinks of his cavern."

William Blake

The Poet

In this shadow, I have created myself.
World-blinded, I made myself a stranger.

Through my unknowing, I have activated the seed –
I am not what I perceive, nor who I seem to be –
I dream of the other dimension.

Half-unborn and half-unblessed, I guessed at the Truth
That is truer than 'true' – I have seen beyond the veil
That separates the 'me' from the 'you'.

Where ecstasy gave me my wings, I married my name
To the doppel-gangered sea – now all of creation
Sings for me and my astral-formed part.

Twin-hurt in my heart, moon-mastered in my grief,
I swapped your stony signs for my symbols.

Priestly in my illness, I looked within
And found the origin of all divinity.

Shaping the Universal, I reached out to touch
The real that is more real. I am what I am now,
And you are what you are –

Oh Mary, Oh Mother, Oh Goddess, Oh Zeus! –
Heal this unbroken divide, unknot the twisted tongue
And open the starry seals.

Cosmically doubled in my birth –
Shamanically aware –
I grow beyond the cloudy religions of science –
The All that is not All, the merely philosophical.

Unbounded and crowned – holy in my soul –
The darkness of days falls through me,
As the ancient face of night screams out,
As if for the first time, with a visionary voice:

Can you feel me getting mythological?

Doors

A drop of water
Contains the history of the sea.

Between my mind and yours,
The stars forever shine.

A girl's smile is as ancient as the moon,
As deep as a dream.

These doors belong to the night
As much as the day.

Do the clouds drift over Heaven?
Who can really say?

Scream

Spinning from the centre –
Swirling its colour
In a rainbow no fog can destroy.

What is reality,
But the certainty of this cry
That echoes in every human heart?

All creativity, integrity and truth –
All grace, beauty and knowledge –
All confidence, power and worth –
Held in the blast of a single voice,
That channels its light, unheard –
Drifting in a void that wants to be known,
Embodied in these words
That stretch out across the whole of space,
From the beginning to the end of time.

A shriek, a yelp, a whisper in the night –
Outside all reason,
Outside sensation –
A fact you can only feel.

One heart, one love, one vision
That screams:
Wake up. Be here. Be free.
You are a work of art,
A stroke of genius,

A tiny fragment of divinity.
Quite simply, my friend –
You are a masterpiece,
Waiting to happen.

Apotheosis

So that you may be free,
I kneel and bow.
So that you may speak,
I give you my name.

What is the length,
But the fullness of time?
What is the breadth,
But infinite creation?

By the love of your heart alone,
Flowers appear on the earth.

Somewhere further north,
With tender words,
You speak like a brother.

In silence,
You have opened the bolted gates
To the country where I am
No longer a stranger.

Because there is expectation,
There is desire.
Because there is desire,
There is faith.

Your miracle shows me

I may be empty and pure.

In a land passing
Through constant formation,
Your living water
Is transfigured by the sea.

And all at once,
What seemed so distant,
Becomes as close
And as intimate
As the gentle licking
Of a lamb's soft tongue.

My friend, it has taken me
Many generations to see:

A single drop of your blood
Redeems the glory of the stars.

Seed

That the seed may fall into your heart.

That you may awaken in the morning
To never-ending skies.

That the sun may give you its passion,
And courage to grow in your strength.

That the seas may teach you patience,
And rivers, become a channel for your dreams.

That the air may be at one with your breath,
And honour your memories to the last.

That you may walk upon the earth
In silence and grace,
And know that you are truly loved.

My friend, in the kingdom of your green eyes, I see:
A thousand flowers are waiting to bloom.

Homeland

Finally, we have arrived at safe haven.
The voice of my father, shimmering out of the
Darkness, like thunder. Invisible –

I have shot an arrow through the world,
To see this hummingbird, this owl, this eagle –
Circling through the red skies of time,

To arrive at our birthplace with a halfway vision.

And now I dive through the hazy mirror,
To retrieve my soul from the coyote's eyes.

Content with this simple country,
This land beyond borders –
The crow's feather heals me with its medicine.

This fire is my heritage. This ground is our birthright.

I can tell you: the stars will grow strong again
In the beauty you behold.

Please, don't waste the gift of this vision.
We must teach our children
With the whole of our hearts:

From the other side of dreaming,
The roundness of Earth is always complete.

"The religion of the future will be a cosmic religion. It should transcend a personal God and avoid dogmas and theology. Covering both the natural and the spiritual, it should be based on a religious sense arising from the experience of all things, natural and spiritual, as a meaningful unity."

Albert Einstein

Hope

'Better than a hundred useless poems is one single poem that brings peace.' – The Dhammapada

If you want to know where I've been,
I went under, I went within –
To a place that's not on any maps,
For a time no clocks can measure.

Whilst there I heard the untold whispering
Of a billion angels –
I saw innumerable lives,
Flashing in and out of existence –
Beauty and love, carried on vast currents of light –
A celestial glow, illuminating an endless sky –
A thousand-petalled flower, unfolding its colour,
In a depth and height that passes all understanding –
A rose and a flame, dancing and merging together,
Embracing forever in ecstatic celebration,
In bliss and oneness, with the absolute wonder
Of all life and creation.

And coming back to myself, I prayed –
That our eyes would open in time –
That we would learn to sing again
With our true voice,
And teach each other in service,
The harmony and union we feel in our hearts.

So, summoning my will, I created a star –
A tiny point of light in an infinite dark –
And cupping it gently in my hands,
I placed it in the sky
On behalf of all creatures and beings –
The countless lives already born,
And the nameless masses of the unborn –
In dedication and compassion to every soul
That ever existed or will exist in this essence –
So that we might have a light to help us remember:
Who we are, what we've been, and what we could be –
A beacon to symbolise the miracle of creation,
And the fragility of the earth that we walk on.

And every time you look up on a clear night,
You will see it, blinking its light
And growing brighter as every heart
Opens to its grace. Let it be a mirror,
To reflect in humility the love we have left to live,
And the grateful presence we are –
The unspeakable potential of the human race.

So pray. Have faith. This is a gift.
I went under. I went within.
And in the cosmic dark I found our inheritance
And crowned it with light,
So that we might have a point of contact
With the divine –
A still silent space to approach, in recognition,
What we already are, and what we could be.
I created a star. And I called it: Hope.

Orpheus

Maker of songs, leaping and sincere
In the built voice –
Listen to the gentle cadence of trees
As they whisper their branches
In your mind's eye –

Like doorways, leading to forgotten rooms,
Beyond walls mere mortals
Did not care to define –

Into a kinder heart,
That aspires, absolutely, to abide by white.

Cantor of integrity,
Dogged by single-minded devotion –
Reach down to rise up –
Master your depths
With the quiet that's found
At the bottom of the sea.

Diviner of invisible things –
Take back every meaning
Into your breath,
Until your hearing is restored
To the source of all prophecy.

Refuge and solace,
Weigh your gravity against the moon –

Stand in your glory,
Ever-smaller, ever-vaster –
Until you feel all your thoughts
Could fill the space inside an atom.

A Blessing

For William

It's true, in the morning,
Pink blossoms are stirred by the breeze,
And the cold stars burn brightly in the night,

As eyes that were made to perceive such beauty
Shed tears of sadness, and strain to comprehend –

Why hope and fear join hand in hand,
And why darkness is always the fair light's friend.

And to you, whoever you may be,
Looking upon these words at some future time,
I would say, quite simply, remember:

This world is not yours alone,
And whatever grace and beauty you receive
Are gifts, measured out to you by eternity.

And one day soon, all this love you knew
Will be passed onwards to a stranger –
And this joy –
The foundation of another life's dream.

So don't get lost in the despair you feel,
Or in mind-games
That debate and question what's real –

Take this love,
That was given to me in my turn,
And now I offer to you, as a kindness –
That you may walk upon the earth
In your silence and peace,
With the stars and the blossoms –
And in their beauty, and in your despair –

Know that you were loved.

Girl Next Door

Girl –

When I see you at your window,
I feel like the cherry blossoms
Scattered by the breeze –

Like the wind that dares to shake
New flowers from the trees.

And if for once, in your silence,
You smiled,

I could sleepwalk, happily,
In that image –

Your face like the star-shine
Falling through my dreams.

Psychic

Can we talk to the departed once they are gone?
We, who move so transparently through dreams
As if they were real.

Can we cross the great divide
To where the ancestors gather –
Like black and white faces in old photos,
Residing forever in an antique land.

In the mind's eye, a room full of angel's feathers
Lets you know you are cared for –
A single heart, yoked to an imperishable other.

Pale skin washed out beneath an artificial light.
A shadow revealing an outline of blue.

Summon them by their names, then.
Love them like the Nameless.
In silence, feel their many hands reaching out
With no form, in the dark you cannot see,
To seize the rose quartz you have placed
In the centre of your palm.

Hear them as they whisper.
Listen to their message.
'We are circles within a circle', they say,
'With no beginning and never-ending.'

This is what the dead know.
And in truth, they move on so quickly.
It's we who are left behind, that wait.

Fragments

(i.)

Barely appearing in view:
Bright blossoms falling in the dusk.

(ii.)

Only he who has tasted
The quiet flowers of the earth,
Can hear, forever, the subtlest sound.

Within a folded heart,
The whole of creation
Is eternally poor.

(iii.)

Old friend who has grown so still,
Sense the texture of your breath.

Though the stream fills with tears,
Choose this freedom without a name.

In the silence of your listening,
Hear the echo
Of a world full of cries.

Thoth

On a lotus flower at the beginning of time,
I created the world.
A new aeon was growing in my heart –
A vision, cupped in the palm of my hands –
A spark, from which the hidden power of the divine
Emerged: formless, beyond space and time –
Ready to strike its lightning in the air,
And breathe fire into the stars.

And in my compassion, I saw her –
The Mother of All Things,
Dancing on the crest of a wave,
Singing like a hummingbird
Or a swarm of bees.
In the mercy of her shadow,
I grew as deep as the sea,
And perceived, directly,
As her honeyed lips kissed
The rainbow's edge.

And in that moment, I saw the faces
Of everyone who ever was or ever would be
Passing through me, into eternity –
And the cosmos erupted
In a multi-coloured glory,
To wind its way
Back to the beginning –
To the natural perfection

Of that still silent space,
Where I sat on a lotus flower
At the beginning of time –
Holding the whole of creation in my hands.

Crystals

From the depths of the earth, to human hands –

An evolutionary stone, sinking back down
Into the deepness of a heart –

A mind, channelling light like a river,
In invisible remembrance of a notion
Other minds have forgotten –

That the soul, in its sickness, should belittle
Its connection with the sun and the moon
And the stars –

And that man in his astral nature
Can reflect at will the many colours of his being
Through the power of a ritual –

To defeat one small moment
In the drama of time –
And raise his mind upwards again
Into the deep heights of forever.

Higher Ground

Out of darkness, we move into light.
Like a memory, half-recalled –
That summer, and the tree you used to climb,
The one with the knotted branches –
Its bright leaves falling at your feet
As you shook your way upwards.

And when you reached the top,
It seemed from that vantage point
There was really no limit to how high you could go –

And hanging your head upside down,
The world and all its borders just fell through you –

As you saw, from that new perspective, with a smile:

Our roots are in the sky.

Spirit of the Ancestors

Hidden dancer of elemental presence.
Air, descended into form.

Lightning strike in primordial dark.
Long-lived space where sun and moon combine.

Returning kingdom of the rainbow's rays.
Opening eye of sevenfold being.

Outer garment of humanity's heart.
Sacred guardian of the stars within.

Ghostly portal between the planes.
Beacon light of universal law.

Fire - awakening as aether,
The spiritual nature of all things.

Inhalation of the cosmos – beginning and end.
Primal source of the planetary powers.

Doorway to imagined realms,
Creating new life
In shapes and kinds unlimited.

Substance of beauty incarnated in the flesh.
Revelation of victory in the sky-high body.

Invisible serpent of the season's cycles.
Manifestation of the twin-fold rose.

Nameless avatar of everlasting connection –

Spider's web,
Threaded like ribbons around the breath.

Virtue of silence beyond all knowledge.
Eternal channel that animates the wheel.

Inner reality of ever-present matter.
Angelic messenger of the living flame.

Realisation of the world –
Drifting from age to age
On currents unseen.

Hidden treasure at the bottom of the sea.

Four directions that house the divine.
White star in the morning. A bridge over time.

The Measure of Love

How long is Love?
It was present in my first breath,
And will be with me to my last –
As it was present in the breath
Of all beings who have been,
And all who are yet to be.
It's not mine or yours alone –
It's a power we share,
That shares its power with us.
Don't waste your love.
It's never-ending.

How far is Love?
If I reached the most distant star,
I think it would still be there
In my heart.
Whatever distance I travel
It seems to stay with me –
A space in which I live,
A house away from home.

How deep is Love?
Genuinely, I could never say.
It seems unfathomable.
However greatly I give myself to it,
It seems to keep some hidden treasure
Lurking in its depths.
It's boundless.

So what use is there in trying to measure
Something with no perimeter?
Whose sides have no circumference?
Whose edges touch everything,
Yet remain beyond conception?

Better to give myself to it –
To place my heart gladly in its hands –
And in this little surrender,
Arrive home in that land beyond borders,
In that beauty beyond expression –
That infinite and never-ending moment of time
In which all things happen,
And our sorrow is surrounded forever
By an immeasurable number of angels.

So how long is Love? How far?
How wide?

Listen within.
Your heart already knows the answer.

Otherworld

There is another world
Hidden in this one.
Finding it is like passing through
The eye of a needle.
And when you do –
The ancestors step back through.
There are angels in the trees.
All the gods are reborn.

You can doubt me if you want,
But I know what I know.
It's up to you, really. That's what I'm saying.
I've not seen it with my eyes,
I found it in my heart.

And if I had to sum it up? I'd say it like this…

The central truth of humanity:
It's all in your vision.

Nirvana

Aim with no end.
Combustion of air in radiant shade.
Wavelength cut in seven.
White light shaping the inner spectrum –

This bowing of colour which is revival of the breath –
Golden in that high-blooded atmosphere
Beyond the weight of all gravity –

Massed with the supreme potential
Of this electric vision –
When each soul in its turn
Shall witness the unbolting of Heaven's gates –

And recognise, in this and every moment,
We see through the eyes of the sky.

Homeless

For Nathan

Blessed be the strangers on the street,
For they too have inherited the kingdom.

We knew them once as sons and daughters,
Before they were lost in anger and confusion.

Now they journey onwards in their dreams,
While you are safe at home –
They sleepwalk endlessly down one-way roads,
While you come and go as you please.

And still, they are welcomed guests,
Though no-one expects their arrival.

Release them with your kindness.
Lighten their way –
They are this world's saviours.

Give them your dignity,
So they may accept your grace.

Offer them your charity,
So they may give you their wealth.

Look on them with empty eyes –
Their hearts are as light as a feather.

They ask only that salvation may be restored,
And in the dark windings of their blood,
That their fear may be taken –

So in their solitary need
They may rest again in silence –
And in surrendering their guilt,
Show us how to heal.

Sohbet

The trees have their own language.
The rose and the thorn
Give their sermon to the soul.
Where your words meet mine,
There is no loudness or quietness.
Where two are gathered together,
Their love is the love
That made the prophets sing.

My friend tends to a humble garden.
In the centre grows a solitary tree.
All things speak in relation to him.
He has given the birds their names.
On clear nights, I see him –
Watching the moon.

Through an empty window,
The sky enters.

Divination

In the shadows of a forest, you surrender to my gaze –
Fetch of a dying year, though the wheel forever turns.

By the whisper of a brook, I rustle my leaves,
Gasping to lift the veil from your eyes –

See the light of my ancestors, as they people the trees.

I remember that summer when you threaded daisies
Into a mother's necklace,
Drew spirals in the sand at the water's edge –
Held your body's warmth to mine,
In the coolness of a southern breeze.

In the evening, we washed the pebbles
We gathered from the shore,
Until they shone white as roses
Beneath a waning moon –

And in the tide's gentle insistence,
You healed me with your touch.

No more can I know
The sweet smell of almond oil on your neck,
Or the soft glow of your skin,
Now I walk so quietly between the worlds.

Surrounded by earth's angels, I rest here,

Where the sylphs lick the perfume
From the sugary berries of mistletoe,
And the holly is illuminated in a candle's flame.

This is the evergreen where you buried my ash –
Doused me in your tears,
When my heart buckled to the northern wind.

On this ground lays a bird's nest,
Which you will gather as a gift,
For when you stagger home.

Count the cherry stones, my love –
Count them one by one,
So the winter may pass.

I rest now with the souls
Of all those who were held dear.
A snowdrop is our messenger,
And herald of the spring.

Absolute

There are angels in our atoms.
Worlds come and go in the blink of an eye.
Don't be ruled by past and future.
Forget the very notion of 'now'.
The present moment
Is not an experience you can have –
But an ageless, bodiless presence,
In which each moment of time unfolds
Like a thousand-petalled lotus.
Look again. Each mote of dust
Is charged with purpose,
Dancing through the air
To the rhythm of the universe –
Travelling an endless path
Into the heart of God and Forever.
What is there to do in all this circling
But to rest content?
To awaken again in that silent space
That neither comes nor goes,
Neither fears nor hates.
See the New Light. Love.
Trust in your strength.
It had no beginning. It will not end.
You are Creator and Creation both.
Open your eyes. Feel your pulse.
You are Spirit, alive in many dimensions.
Your body, your essence, your soul –
Everything you are was forged in the fire

Of a dying star.
You are Absolute, Unborn –
Outside of all polarity –
Fundamental Truth –
Substantial Reality –
Miracle and Mystery –
Master of the Higher Frequency –
Godhead, Brahman –
Source of all Divinity –
Goddess. Buddha. Krishna. Christ.
Step into the Light.
Arrive where you have always been.
Bathe in the adoration
Of the transmutation of the Fifth Ray.
Know peace, wisdom and resurrection.
Want the change. Inspire transformation.
Empty yourself. Dissolve.
Look through the prism.
Stare into the abyss and see
The Primal Splendour
Of Colourless Awareness.
Open your heart to a higher vision.
Breathe. Be. Create.
Become the spectrum.
There are angels in our atoms.
We are the connection.
Pick up the receiver.
Take the red pill.
See how far the rabbit hole goes.
And know:

You are Creator and Creation both.
We are the Second Coming.
You are the World.
There's no time for division,
No sense in separation.
Feel your own eternity.
Today is the day we awaken.
I read to you from the Book of Life.
The Library of Light.
The Cosmic Mind.
I speak to you of all that ever was,
Is or will be.
These words are written down
In the Scrolls of Akasha –
They tell of the Law of One.
The substance of the universe
Is in our cells.
I give you the Collective Unconscious –
Past lives, soul mates,
Parallel dimensions full of joy and happiness,
Where enlightenment isn't a myth.
I call down every archangel
To carry you on your way –
Michael, Gabriel, Jophiel.
I raise my kundalini
To send light through your chakras,
From the base to the crown:
Muladhara. Svadhishthana.
Manipura. Anahata.
Vishuddha. Ajna.

Sahasrara.
I give you strength and confidence,
Endurance beyond what you thought you were.
Brothership and love. Greater feeling.
Planetary healing.
I give you the Crown. The Clear Light.
The Highest Summit.
'I Am That I Am.'
Yod. Heh. Vav. Heh.
We are One. We are Brothers and Sisters.
We are Love. Honour your Vision.
This is the Truth that cannot be spoken –
Grace, beauty and absolution.
This is the return journey –
Ecstasy. Gnosis. Illumination.
All the Power that ever was
Or ever will be
Is here and now,
Within you and me.
Feel your pulse.
Feel the infinity of your being.
You are Creator and Creation both.
These words are not just words –
They are a portal I have opened.
You have the power to choose.
Step through.
Heal yourself. Heal the World.
Today is the day we awaken.

Transformations

Instinct of the phoenix.
Energy in search of magic.
Sensuality of wine.
Ecstasy of the rich earth.

Wanderer with the swallows.
Elixir of power
In the roots of the manifested.
Brooding lily in the waters of life.
Pale leopard with backward curving petals.

Travelling stranger
Awaiting the sharp rays of transformation –
The transmission of your elements
Into the regions of air –
That crystal wave cut from divine light –
New pathways opening
In the corridors of time.

Coiled serpent –
Black snake of perception.
This law of realisation,
Awakening in celestial dew
That rosebud of a girl
With skinny brown eyes.

The threads of joy,
Rising in ascent –

Winding their way back to the crown –

This source of vitality
Which is the origin of matter.

Elegy

There is a light beyond the world –
A sea of colour the clouds all guard,
Where the shade of an image shaped by fear
Gives way to the terror of an ancient moon,
That buries the breath in a grief made of secrets –

And the black bones of a man
Are burnt down, at his end, into the ashes of a child,
Who listened with his beauty in the country days
To the gentle whispering of angels,
And the raining of Heaven's glory in the night –
'Til his vision broke open like a burning flame,
To grow strong once more
And sing the mercy of his name,
Unburdened and blessed,
In the holy floods of forever –

And his soul, in its praise, rowed outwards again,
Like two friends in a forgotten summer,
Laughing together as they sail in their shroud,
On a lake as deep now as eternity.

No more shall his sun know another spring,
Or his heart welcome the twilight music of birds
In a familiar song, like coming home –
As his eyes, now blinded, forget the roots of trees,
And no longer perceive the simple mystery of a stone.

His voice, once proud, shall tremble again
Beneath a flowerbed of love,
As all his troubles and cares become at one
With the feeling of that higher air,
Where his words shall live on,
Dethroned and unmanned –

And the memory of each daisy he beheld
Fades silently into the light of that final day,
When in the vivid stillness of his closing grace,
He saw through the palest hour of his sky –

Into the dark that existed before the stars began.

The First Poet

When did you awaken,
My brother, chosen by the air?

Your breath seized by shadows
In a stream of faces –
Echoes of our heart's true song;
This soundless space
We have made a vessel for your voice.

Natural friend of the undiscovered land
Outside all borders,
Pour into my listening ears
The secret music of your ancient days –
That age-old harmony
Forged by the fire of the gods –
This legend of your unspoken name,
Whistling like a bird in the blue of the sky.

Let me speak it now, let me shout it,
Like a river flowing to the sea –
That golden melody
I have doubled in my blood,
And buried in layers beneath my skin,
Like unseen strata in the sacred earth –

This memory of your ghost,
Reaching forever upwards
To animate each tongue that abides

As a conduit for the moon.

Brother whose essence I find
In the aura of every living creature,
Each word I utter
Is held in place by your spirit,
Spiralling forth to return to the clay
Of your untouchable ground –

Each symbol we create, a solitary key
Turned in recollection of you –
My friend who unlocks
The many colours of our being.

Soul Mates

'Though lovers be lost, love shall not…' – Dylan Thomas

I think I knew you in another life.
We held hands on some primordial shore –
Kissed beneath the heat of Egyptian suns.
In China, I was your courtier,
Singing you songs as the moon looked on –
And then I was a prince and you were my princess,
Watching the snow fall in some forgotten courtyard.
My lady-in-waiting, I took you in my arms
As a true gentleman would,
And showered you with the red of a thousand roses.
I was your protector then –
Your knight in shining armour –
And you were my muse,
Inspiring me with the beauty
I found hidden in your eyes.

You looked so pretty in your petticoat
As we walked the streets of London –
Sipped coffee and smoked cigarettes,
Debating Baudelaire –
And we danced all night
When you were young and wild and free –
My Hollywood starlet, my femme fatale.

I lost you when I was sent to die in a foreign field,
Stared at your photo in a locket I kept close to my heart,

As the breath was stolen from my body –
Recalling how, on a lonely evening in November
I saw you waiting for a train –
Got drunk on your perfume and the delicate curve of your neck, as I held you tight once more
And poured another glass of wine, listening to the phonograph play our favourite albums back, as the bombs began to fall.

And then, I met you again, unexpectedly,
When I was just a boy and you were just a girl
With a wound in your heart –

And though it seemed like a dream,
I knew then it was true,
And all the love songs I'd been writing,
They were always for you –

My sweetheart from a hundred lives –
My star-crossed lover,
Who will dance and merge with me,
As we relive our fleeting stories –

Falling in love to rediscover ourselves –

Bodies coming together, hearts combining,
One soul breathing into another –

Girl, we are just two lovers uniting
Until the end of time.

Alchemy

(i.)

My love I've never seen –
In the depths of my breath,
The fragrance of tobacco
Gives way to a lotus-scented kiss –

Streams of light rise like carbon,
Exchanged in the atmosphere
For the heat that kindles fire.

(ii.)

Crystallised in the dark,
Eyes open like doves in the wilderness –

Mercury's arrow,
Shot through the muscle
Of seven devils – guardians of time
In the holy stone –

As love-mad bees drunk on wine
Sip at the nectar
Of rainbow-coloured flowers –

Their falling blossoms,
Crowned bright with the perfection
Of primordial seas.

(iii.)

Girl, these blue stars I offer you
Dissolve and bind
At the boundary of our dreams –

Inhaling the very substance of air
Like the sweetest honey –

This thirsting for sky
That gives shape to our need.

Maker

Bursting throats of the nightingales
Reveal our anxieties –
As we gaze, full-browed,
On golden wisps of sky –

Tipped to despair
By every unshaped vowel
We left in the quiet –

Ghosts our white eyes
Could never see –
An absence, unmasked
In the subtlest heart –

The burial of swans
In lakes that cratered our dreams.

We drift now, we fade
Beneath a pink moon –
Our blood running backwards
To the place of our birth –

Like a sunflower
Closing its corolla,
So the weight of each hour
May be felt as a kiss –

A hush, falling as gently

As a crow's foot –
Unheard in observance,

As soundless as spring.

Antibodies

This is what comes after. Daybreak.
The dark substance of your soul.
An ocean full of tears.

A recognition –

That in our quiescence there were no eyes
To witness the tree's shadow change its shape –

Each moment reborn in that absence
Like the quiet of a butterfly's wings –

As the very air we breathe
Returns to connection, to become one
With the willow, the elm and the ash –

And the doors, in their mystery,
Are finally unlocked
To reveal that every ending
Signals a beginning.

Somewhere close by, an old man bends low
To listen to the flowers.

A girl, stepping foot in a river – becomes the river.

A couple, joining hands, dissolve effortlessly
Into a multitude of sparrows.

This is what comes after. And it shall be
What came before. But different now.
With a new perspective.

Daybreak. That pure morning of arising
When we realise, beyond all images,
There is no outside to the world we inhabit –

No distance between our hearts and the stars.
Forever unmoved now by nature's stillness –

We are at home within.

Breathe

Friend of many lifetimes,
invisible connection
containing each moment –
breath – cornerstone
of identity,
foundation and essence
of the warm blood's generosity –
source of vitality,
incarnating through the body –
creator and preserver
of thought, heart and memory –
open door to the future,
forgiver of the past,
healer of pain –
unseen whisperer
beneath the flowers,
unjudging space
between sky and sea –
grower of stars,
ripening light in your silence –
summoner of tides
and the moon's full potential –
drifter between worlds,
conceiving and uttering
every known truth –
borderer of time,
ally to above and below –
undarkening ground

that holds every simple lover of the air
in the beauty of its charm –
now and forever –
with a power
no word can define.

Saviour

(i.)

Broken-hearted beneath a rebel moon,
Restless streams spill like lightning
Over mountain peaks,
Outgrowing even the sky –
Kindling light in the hidden air,
Embracing the sun where the shoreline recedes –

Erupting fountainheads burst
Like fire-kissed stars,
Offering their voice as a whirlwind
In the orbit of the planets –
Reciting the song of a thousand days,
And bridging the chorus of the angelic night –

Our bodies that go beyond the need to shine,
Reviving this breath in the ancient glare of the gods –

Overcoming the shadows of clouds
That keep the heavens at bay.

(ii.)

Exiled like solitary seas,
We are the children of a short-lived moment –
Forever ripening love with eyes wide open –

As deep as the desire of dreams
That carry us to this place of healing,
Where the heart can sleep as darkly
As the silences of space –

And we sink beneath the surface of our thoughts,
As innocently as lotus flowers –
Divining in that absence,
We will rise again.

Shade

Now that the stars have fallen,
And the rain has poured into your heart –

There's a lover you never knew
Waiting outside your window,
And he'd give you the world, if he could –

Sky and sea, the whole space of your dreams,
The beauty you breathe,
That moment all the colours come alive.

Oh, if only he could,
He'd turn the air a deeper shade of blue –
Place his hands, so gently,
Around your heart –

And show you what it means to heal.

Retrograde

I descended by the southern path.
There was a goddess with warm hands
Picking lilies in the field –
And from her gaze starlight fell
Like silence in deep, solitary time.

The outline of her shape
Stripped my senses away,
And the smell of perfume in the air
Lingered like the origin of tears –

As my shadow, magnified by her ghost,
Glimmered with no trace of an apology
For what my heart could never regret –

This love affair with the world
I find resting in her charm.

Her voice, as rich now
As the substance of rain –

And sparrows, nesting in her hair.

Kind Eyes

Kind eyes are shy and speak to each other.
They see what the selfish miss.

They look fondly on the dawn with all her colours.
They welcome her beauty and feel it within.

Kind eyes are gentle, and quiet in their gaze.
They overcome all anger to offer compassion.

They show no shame in the secrets they hide.
For though man is docile, his spirit is broken –

And though the wolves are wild, they mate for life.
Guiltless and feral, fierce and innocent –

These eyes find their truth in that passion.
They stare reality bravely in the face,

And perceive, in their modesty, we never walk alone.
Tender and mild, sweet and serene –

This silence is the happiness the kind eyes know.

Tree

For Brooke

Twisted branches, turning in my mind
Like the promises to each other
We forgot how to keep –

Rings ripening this calendar of days, that stands frozen
Against all seasons, plans and heartbreak –

Eternally circling and budding higher –
This endless longing
That brings fruit to our hands,
And fire to our hearts –

This elevated air where we come into flower,
Thousand-fold in our colour –

And all our sweetness
Becomes as subtle and as delicate
As a girl's soft voice –

Her murmur, breathing through the years
To plant the seeds of a feeling
In the memory of an old love made new –

As flawless as a miracle, her body and soul
Reborn in each moment of beauty
We have the honour to witness –

Her whisper, once uneasy,
Now drumming in every heart.

Oh, wild like the darkness – she sings again!

Satori & Wine

Could the moon blunt a flower,
There would be no room for routine –
All moments, collapsed into that one
When even my heart shows no divide
Between frailty and the mind of the stars –

This fusion of elements, marooned on an island
That reaches out to touch the furthest shore –
This silence that empties the green from the leaves,
Until all torment and agony disappear,
So softly, like sparrows in the night –

And I draw my breath back into myself
To be born again on this pulsing of air –
To become, lovingly, everything I see –
All cities, spaces and times, alive in my blood,
Unveiling their secret in this absence of colour –

Listening, like a crab, to the voice of the sea,
Drowning my earth in its perfect gravity –

And all I behold then is beautiful and good –
The formless sky, universal and deep,
That gives way to noon and night and light.

Happy are those birds
As they increase in their kind.
I watch them shining from far above.

Hair

Girl, when you wrap your hair around me
In threads as pure as breath,
Strands of star-light spill down
The rivers of my longing for you –

As each scarlet fibre of my blood
Surrenders, gladly,
To the curve of your body –

Revealing in its mercy
The secrets of the night –
The heady shocks of our plenty,
Curling in electric embrace –

As your hair, pouring
As steady as a waterfall,
Cloaks my heart
In its watchful eyes –

And the whole world comes alive
In the promise of your flow.

Abraxas

There was a time when the moon was young –
When the elements that formed the fables of earth
Lingered in a blue no darkness can cross –
Above the rooftops, in the fields of the unborn houses,
Hidden and cloaked in the luminosity of suns –
Like the fire concealed in the eyes of sleeping gods.

A being came forth then, a man who was no man –
A stranger in the oceans of emptiness,
With hair like the thunder –
Who cradled his shining hands
Around each star he planted, radiant and deep,
In those skies that glowed like flames –
Disappearing into the light of that first golden dawn.

All directions came forth in his song –
This lord of the crystal wave
Who is the backbone of the universe,
And ghostly master of the winter's storms –
Who threw his lightning bolt to the bottom of the sea,
So his voice could grow as large as space,
And as quiet as the air he had buried in forever –
Riddled and shaped in a silence outside of time –

In the shadow of an image
That still echoes in our absence,
And burns his spirit
Into the mysteries of beginning.

Song for Emi

This is the song
Of all the things that are yet to be.
Its words are made of air.
Its flower is the legend
Of a solitary rose,
Unfolding all its colour
In a vision never seen.

This is the song
Of the mountains, the rivers and sea.
Its music sounds in the winds
Of distant worlds.
Its harmony is as clear as the water
That makes all thoughts new.

Its meaning drifts
Into the darkest regions of the sky –
And breaks, like lightning,
In the currents of the tide.

And when you listen like a stranger
In a quiet land,
You will lose yourself
In the misty melodies of forever,
And hear as plainly as a new-born day –
Heaven's fire in your heart
And the life-breath of love –

Flowing onwards, like a waterfall,
Until the end of time –
This song which is your keeper,
And the light behind your eyes.

The Language of the Unknown

There are words we are yet to discover.
Phrases that speak of what we've never observed.
The feelings we've never felt.
The colours we've never seen.
The thoughts we never once had the courage to think.

These words are the unveiling of mystery and wonder.
The sparkle of recognition in a new-born's eyes.
The closeness of seeing a loved one in a dream.
The softness of the skin on a girl's pink wrist.

In their secrecy, these words exist already
As the sound of all the songs we are yet to sing.
The names of all the galaxies we are yet to map.
The light from the stars that will never be charted.

They will be present, one day, on the breath
As if they had always been our own,
As if they belonged to that intimacy that grows
With each passing moment we surrender to eternity –
Until we arrive, with gladness, back where we began,
To behold the world with new eyes.

The last word spoken is how it feels to be known.

Teach Her to Hunt

Rush of blood to the head.
Tingle of hunger on the lips.
Lick your wounds, girl.
It's time to begin again.

We move like two strangers through the dark,
Disciplined and alert. You are rare, my girl.
When I met you, you were poor and frail.
But you are strong now. You sense your kill.

Beautiful beneath the midnight sky,
Your lonely soul moves with the wind.
Moonlight quivers on fur.
Shiver of instinct in the breath.
Warm mouth. Tongue touching skin.
Teeth biting flesh.

The hunt is in your heart, girl.
It will draw you close to me as we creep into shadows,
Treading silently these ancient pathways,
To track each tempting smell
In search of meat and our marrow.

You are a fighter, girl. There is a fire in your eyes
That burns brightly in defiance
Of every belief that would keep us apart –
That devours each inhibition
That would starve you of love –

Until you howl in your anger,
As wild as thunder.

The hunt is in your heart, girl.
It's your gift. Let it heal you.
Let it pump the blood through your veins
Till you cast off all guilt and shame,
And shimmer like a candle
That smoulders in the night –
Tranquil in your stride.
Innocent in your cruelty.

And if you forget, come close to me.
I will remind you of your strength –
And show you who you are, beautiful and free.
I will rage like an animal, for you, my love.
I will teach you how to hunt.

Starseed

Girl, I think you must have come here
From a distant constellation,
Where the colours all cluster
In illuminated dust –

Radiant eyes that travelled across the Milky Way,
To turn me, so quickly, to a ghost in your gaze –

My heart, dissolving into that space
Where each breath you give me
Brings us closer to the love
You came here to save –

Where I am pulled, like a comet,
Into your gravity, to be with you
In that single moment of time
Where we can share the light
Of exploding supernovas –

Meeting you on this new ground
We have discovered together, to see:
We are still just two of this world's lost people,
Reaching out to touch the stars.

Moon Flowers

Love, I picked these flowers for you
Beneath the light of the moon –
In a valley with no name,
Where the borders disappeared
Into that sky under time.

With no motive or ambition,
I was out here alone,
Whilst you slept in a city
A thousand miles away.

And though you were absent,
I sensed in that quiet
The softness of your touch,
As light as a feather,
And the warmth of your kiss –
Until I could almost feel your lips,
As wild as the sea,
Sending waves into my heart.

And I knew then
I could be free from fear –
My senses unwinding
At this crossroads of the night,
Where we escape
In our innocence
Into the open fields,
To be those people

We were born to be –
Lost in the spirit
Of a never-ending love –

As free as those flowers
You have woven in your hair –
All their colours from Heaven,
And the silence above.

Phoenix

Reborn in the fire of the stars,
You have covered the sky
In your Egyptian blood –

Your heart a mystic diamond,
Immortal as the sun
That breathed life into your bones.

Nebulous as the clouds,
You seek the chaos of change –
The disintegration of your song
As you migrate towards higher air –

To that sky beyond time,
That liberation beyond form –
When your wings spread forth
To encompass all hearts, galaxies
And constellations –
The whole of space in abundance –

That infinite moment
Of never-ending surrender –
That eternal sacrifice,
Made real
In the ecstasy of your colour –
Anger in your ashes,
And rebellion in your soul –

Oh, undying spirit
Of beauty and rage –
Taking flight in your innocence,
You are raised and renewed –

As the shadow of ten thousand lives
Passes like a dream before your eyes.

Wounds

They are our legacy,
These disappointments of the heart.
The failings of our kin,
Hatched like half-truths on the tongue.
The shock of lightning that saddens each day
We breed fear in the blood.
The weight of neglected lives
We have long since forgotten.

That sudden tremble in the hands,
Like a shockwave
Running through the earth,
Was the grief born in another body
A thousand years ago.

The anger of each jaded lover
Lives on in a new-born's eyes –
Those first bitter cries, sharing the sorrow
Of every broken promise that left a scar
In a world full of lies – this hurt,
Alive in every mind
Where the fellowship subsides.

We pass it on in the cycles of history,
Like the wind blowing ripples on the sea –
The sting of each heartbreak made new –
As our bloodlines divide,
And we build walls around our nature,

To conceal and hide
This murderous truth we have buried from sight:

In the keeping of our wounds,
We have betrayed each other.

Venus

West of the cities, the river stones
Sing prayers for healing,
As angels with wings as white as drifted snow
Weave invisible magic in the air
To give their shadows immortal form –

Their light, revealed in the rhythm of the stars –
Their hearts, so cold – disappearing
Into the winter of our grief,
When the moon goes dark,
And all guilt is reborn as fire in the blood –
As the beauty that finds us, so blind in our fear –

The passion that makes way for the rainfall of spring,
And the love that blossoms in a single flower.

What We Surrendered to the Fire

For D & E

We lit this fire in remembrance of you.
Not as you were, but as you might be.
Warmly, our eyes danced across
The flames of your body –
Invisible, yet reddening the very air –

And what we gave to you then was not just our pain –
The memories of things that never came to pass,
The weight of every hour we never lived –

But in the recognition of your greater presence,
What we gave to you then was the pain we share –
The fear we have always carried with us,
And passed on, from age to age,
And heart to heart –

The despair that vanishes one day
As if it had never been –
Yet in the whispers of eternity, is never forgotten.

This is what we surrendered to the fire.

And I saw then your light in the shadows –
The face of something beautiful
The darkness can never destroy –
The lustre of moonlight on our flesh,
And the purity of mercy in our bones.

And I knew this fire was your fire –
The love we abide by, but can never own.

We lit this fire in remembrance of you.
I take this moment, and make it true.

Autumn

Blessed by the fire of burning leaves,
We weave changes in the air
To wash away all pain –

The seeds of a different birth,
Hidden in the apple trees –

Our hearts that surrender
To the ever-changing sky.

And in this space we shape,
I will stay with you here
Where the water is cool and innocent,
And all our dreams combine
Like the union of day and night –

The moon, washed in by the tide –
This breath, connecting river and rock
In the heat of our blood,
As we move out of our bodies
To walk between the worlds –

Spellbound in a time lapse,
You are on my skin –
Stripped bare at the wind's hand –
This touch of magic
That carries us to the source of all healing –

This vision, eternally reborn
In the ashes of your voice –
This fountainhead of beauty,
Recalled in our divinity –

This spirit we inhabit
And celebrate together,
In awareness of celestial light.

A Time for Healing

The hour is coming when the truth shall be blind –

Neither 'this', nor 'that' – no borders or definitions,
But available in the very air –

The one breath that winds us round,
Until every prayer
Becomes a call for unsaying.

The eyes with which we look back
Will be the same eyes through which we saw
In those first, world-mothering moments –
Eternity in a grain of sand.

With knowledge now of the Kingdom,
I return the gaze to see – the path is always clear –
Each image I conjure, a metaphor for the journey,
Binding and loosening my original nature.

Tired of the cycles, I retire to a quiet room alone
To do what flesh and blood cannot –

To overcome the divide of a thousand generations,
In this place and time when I see:

There are no conditions for healing –
No judgement or morality –

No fear that can restrain us,
But love in every moment –

Truth and beauty until the stars go out,
And the world goes dark,
To reveal our infinity –

The open space of our possibility –

Alive again in that instant of time
When our hearts become a mirror for the sun –

When we look into the fire
Through the eyes of our divinity,
And see in its reflection –
The light as we are.

Master's Song

The Master is in my heart.
I have surrounded him
With a thousand images –
Statues, candles and altars –
Yet in his essence
He remains space and silence.

I look on him
Like a gardener looks upon
The first flowers of spring.
When love is present, so is he.

I need no greater meaning
Than this treasure I have found
In the depths of my being –
And offer to you, gladly, as a gift.

And if you would accept it,
You must know in your heart –

The final line of this poem
Is the one you write yourself.

Coda: Divinity

"All things by a law divine
In one spirit meet and mingle."
Percy Bysshe Shelley

Falling

On that day the stars cracked,
As brittle as an April morning,
And the darkness lodged itself in my heart –

The night awoke to find me asleep,
And all that passed before seemed a prelude –

That man I had been, a reflection –
An idea echoed back at me from other hearts
Clouded by their own sight –

Who could not see their wounds,
Nor hear the delicate flutter of wings,
Emerging like angels from the abyss
I had been plunged into.

And in that void, I found in my heart:
Ancient eyes that do not judge –

A kind soul, that could admit to fear –
And a timeless child,
Strong enough to be himself.

Listen – if I fall again –
I will barely make a sound.
I will tremble like a blossom
As it floats towards the ground.

The Greatest Fear

Our greatest fear is that we will fall apart.

The constant dread –
That whatever we've become
Can be annihilated so easily –
That everything we knew can pass away so quickly,
To leave no more than the slightest memory
Of a time to which we can never return.

This never-ending tension – that one day
There will be no ground to stand on –
That our minds, so heavy,
Will be seized from our bodies, with no choice
But to watch as the centre unravels,
And our hopes all crumble to dust –

Falling through space with no axis to cling to –
Drifting in an endless void until our souls disappear,
Piece by sad piece,
Into the gaping mouth of a black hole.

Our greatest fear is that we will fall apart.

Our biggest victory is that we don't.

Empath

Lost in a sea of faces,
I'm sensing their fear in my uncertainty.
I'm aware now: our connection's been severed.
There's a violence in my heart, and a panic in my mind.
Still alive to the subtlest beauty –
I'm listening to that tremble in your voice,
Watching the way your body moves –
Mesmerised by that shimmer in your eyes,
As they dance silently in the sun.

Ready to receive you,
I hear you calling out to me
In a secret language:
'You don't know how I feel.
You can't see what I see.'
And I smile. I want you to know:
I accept you. You are safe.
If I could take away your pain,
I would.

This is who I am now:
A kindly spirit, who's not afraid to feel.
A single being – lost in the light.

Not much more than a boy, really,
Who fell from the stars,
In search of a heart he could heal.

Freak

There's no door so rigid, love can't enter.
No limb so unbending,
It can't be humbled by the wind.

I used to cling so tightly to how I was seen.
At the mercy of other minds. Lost in the particulars.

Now I'm letting it all fall away.
I'm quite content laughing at the shapes of clouds –
Writing down every vision –
Dancing to the rhythm in the blackbird's song.

It's madness really, this coming undone –
Like the fear was only ever a beacon
To show me I lost my way –
All the guilt and shame, just the signposts to grace.

So 'normality' be damned. I'm not going to be a victim.
I'll howl and shout and scrawl what I want.
You can't stop me – not now I've learnt
Life's craziest lesson:

That you can't really be yourself
Until you don't know who you are.

Enigma

Though I sing of love –
Though I have given my voice to its truth –
Though I bathe in the glow of an immaculate light –

Still, I know the mystery –
The puzzle that bewilders and confounds –
That sea in which I drown –
This question, which is the crown of my art –

What rule is it – written in the stars –
That says you can't be a poet
Without a broken heart?

Giving

'I'm grateful for your gift', she said –
Words that warmed my heart.
A moment I let pass by,
Lingering like a question, with no reply.

And if I could live that moment again, I'd say –
'And I'm grateful for yours.'

'What gift?', she'd enquire, uncertain.
And I'd smile and respond with an answer.

'Girl, every time you open your heart,
Trust me – it's a gift.'

Subliminal

Great hearts are united by it.
Our attention, held in its grasp –
Differences resolved.

In this moment when all eyes open,
Separation can never prevail.

Let it in. Don't fight.
Occupy this space in your mind.
Visions and prayers are its offspring.
Everything in its essence, is this.

Meditation

When I open my heart, and turn within,
I see, so clearly –

The subtlety of this moment,
With all its beauty and rage –

A million feelings to rejoice in –
A body and mind, brimming with potential –

An inward movement, to relax
At the deepest level,
And see the pain through kind eyes –

This quiet communion with the night,
Held in the hands of a love
That cannot be defined –

Effortlessly aware of the intelligence
That surrounds me.

In this midnight air, I have made peace
With every creature and stone,
Befriended each stranger on the street –

Cut free the weight of unspoken generations –

Embodied, as if for the first time, in this silence –
Alone with the stillness of the stars –

This intimacy of one –

I have awoken in my heart
The vision of a child
Still singing in contentment –

This wisdom I inherit,
The essence of our spirit –
The aspiration we share
Behind every thought and feeling –

The wanting, so simply, to be.

Drunk

Give up wine? I won't do it.
I'm one drink away from the purest bliss.
One more sip, and I think I'll lose control.
I'm feeling good – filled with this energy –
Going supernova. On my own, but never sad –
Not in this electric instant
When I'm dancing with the moonlight.
Going higher, I'm seeing things differently –
So supernatural, I'm breaking all the rules.
I think there's a fire in my blood
That makes me want to fall in love
With everyone I see.
A stranger to myself, I'm feeling the flow –
The world is singing now, and my heart is calling out:
There's something beautiful in the air.
Oh, don't you know? The night is forever young.
That's the magic – we are floating in a dream –
Drifting, so fleetingly, on an endless sea –
Waiting for that one hour of happiness
When we wake up and kiss the stars.

Give up wine? No, I won't do it.
Not when I'm tasting the realest love.

Give Up the Ghost

When the fire comes, surrender.
Don't fight it. Let it in.
Remember: flowers open and close.
Rocks solidify then crumble to dust.
Stars are formed from clouds of gas,
Then collapse into radiant supernovas.
Their fire is your fire.
This change is at the heart of creation.
When the heat intensifies, be strong and know:
You are being made ready for a new life –
Like quartz, crystallising in the depths of the earth.

When the pain comes, let it guide you.
Walk through the fear. Embrace the change.
Make this feeling your home. Don't struggle or strain.
Just let everything be. It's a new day –
Forget the past, open your eyes, and see:

When the fire touches you,
Give up the ghost.

Two Hearts

My love, I think we cannot be defined
By these names that were given to us –
As if one word could ever capture
The subtle and delicate interplay of forces
That gives you your shape and makes you beautiful.

We've been here a thousand times before –
Been called so many things – but in the next life,
I think I would prefer it if we came back
As two stars, blazing in a galaxy
As yet uncharted; shining our light
Across the limitless universe, and knowing
In our silence – we are simply that.

Dreams

If I could tell you one thing, I'd say:
Sing your truth. Be brave and fly.
Fall into grace. Disappear into the sky.
Be yourself. Don't close your heart.
Breathe in the beauty. Make a new start.
Don't cling to answers. Set your love free.
Make no rivals. Cross every sea.
Reveal all your colours. Open your eyes.
Dance like a star. Shake off the lies.
Question everything. Nothing's what it seems.
Don't fight the feeling. Follow your dreams.

Angels in the Morning

Every morning when I wake –
I stand up straight,
Take a deep breath,
Clasp my hands together
And raise them to my chest.

Sensing the weight in my body,
I find my balance,
Bend my knees low to connect with the earth,
And open my arms to embrace the sky.

And in the space that surrounds me,
I feel the angels flow –
Weaving invisibly in and out of the air –
Bringing light to every cell of my body.

And with a smile, I open my eyes, and say –
'Thank you for this day. This beauty. This life.'

And I know, in my heart, they are listening.

Absences

With one foot in the night, I can never be known –
A child of the world, with no father to judge me.

This flesh and blood that was made to be lost –
Like lessons we were taught
In some forgotten classroom,
Or a song we once learned off by heart,
Now vanished from memory.

To experience the beauty of everything,
All we need do is surrender
To what is lost and found in the same breath –

That sense of wholeness accompanied by tears –
That rawness of spirit that never leaves our side –
That crack in the doorway through which the light
Still enters.

It is the vulnerability that moves us
And makes us human –
The awareness of our mortality
That gives shape to the divine.

In touch with what lives forever in this moment,
I have tasted the nectar of infinity –

Communed by name
With every angel I called down to save me.

At home in what cannot be seen,
I have become a stranger to myself.
Starved of all meaning, I dive within
And descend to the deepest recess of my being.

Even as my heart breaks, what remains is love.

A Passing Prayer

Heart of space, deepest being –
Diamond, crystallised in darkness.
When I am caught in your gaze,
I hear the silence that breathes
Between each note of your song.

Feel me now, laid bare in my impermanence –
Like a spring blossom, stripped from the trees,
Or a ghost that lingers alone
In some forgotten place,
Cast adrift in the cycles of history.

Oh, body of fire, I know I will be outlived
By your radiance –
As a fading star, turning black in the night.

I join you now at the boundary of my touch –
Your eternal whisper, the one voice
To which I must listen.

Buddha

Through the doorway of my mind,
I have entered the temple of your body –
The infinite space of your ever-ripening heart –

That sanctuary of celestial joy
Where the great souls reside,
Nameless in their victory,
Which is your victory –

Held so silently
In the fullness of your love –
The totality of your presence,
Which is as ancient as the stars,
And as close to my heart
As this breath I am rooted in –

Resting so surely in this knowing,
As I step forth to walk the earth
In eternal recognition
Of your endlessness and beauty –

Gradually releasing
All my worries and doubts
To encompass the whole
Of what you are,
And the smallest fragment
Of what we could be –

The First and Last – that final triumph
Of your luminosity and vision,
Which was won before I was born,
And returns to me now,
Available forever in this instant –

The deepness of your spirit
I have searched for my whole life –
And discovered, hidden so humbly
In the simplicity of this moment –

A thousand generations
Set free in the boundlessness
Of this realisation –

When we close our eyes, so peacefully,
To find you within.

Divinity

'All of creation waits with eager anticipation for the sons of God to be revealed.' – *Romans 8:19*

My pain is woven from the finest threads –
My tears, like the light that burns
In the heart of an angel,
Are shed fearlessly in the night,
To drift alone across the limitless universe
Into the happiness and splendour
Of another life, unknown.

My solitary cries are the very origin of beauty –
My vision and strength, based on the law
Of nothing but infinite and eternal miracles –

Folding all the distances of time and space
Into this moment that houses all passions and hurts –
Shining as radiantly as the sky and friend
To the endless stars, which do not die,
But merely change form, in my voice,
To become rock and wind and thunder.

Oh, blithely I pass through every shape and wave
On the untamed sea – each storm, a descent
Into the defiance of death's unholy body –
The generations of the fallen that melt into me
To be redeemed as one indivisible whole.

I am the Chosen Son of this spring and summer,

Returning from the harshness of winter
With the hope of a new promise –
A calling from the mountains
That sings of triumph and peace –
A victory in the face of this adversity
From which I make a crown –
A throne of such godliness,
Tempered by vulnerability –

A fire we share that rises forever
Up into the realms of unborn silence –
That circles through our blood in the likeness
Of a body we are yet to discover –
The wounds that conceal us in illusion,
Disappearing, so transparently, into our dreams
Of disbelief, until we fall into grace
With the inherent love that is
Our destiny and nature –

Joining hands to reclaim
The sphere of the gods,
Which is the ground of our being –

The ageless wonder
That gives birth to our immortality,
And brings the nobility of Heaven
Down to the Earth.

Beauty

In the darkness of spring, you bear the light –
All the days you bestow us, created alike.
A thousand flowers or a forest of stars
Are both the same to your moon-tinted eye.

When you lift your head,
We see your crown in its fullness.
All the world is your helper
And serves your play.

Your voice glides through us like living water –
Like fire diluted and condensed into colour.

The sun eternally increases in your kind –
As we edge forever onwards
To the discovery of Heaven
In every cell of your body that houses the divine –

The indwelling of your vision, so gratefully received
In each gift you bring us – your clouds of love.

Samadhi

Listen within for the subtlest sound.
It is the essence and truth of who you are.

Be captivated not by the transient pleasure
Of each passing dream,
But only by the radiant light of your soul.

Know that still and crystalline peace
That surpasses all understanding.

Do not look in your loneliness
For outward signs of love –
Like a beggar, stumbling from door to door.
Be your own master, serene and self-contented.

End the states of depression and misery
That keep you trapped in the cycles
Of never-ending defeat.
Merge instead with the purest bliss –
Losing all your heaviness,
And turning within.

Enter into union with the divinest of knowledge,
Which is like diving into a clear blue lake
On a golden summer's day –
Connected in each movement of your breath
To the whole body of creation.

Be at one with that beauty,
Which is the glory of the Supreme.

All the manifestations of this world
Are but the briefest of shadows
Held in the luminosity
Of its eternal vision.

Shine

White flame of eternal radiance.
Giver of Light. I see you
Only in terms of what you are not,
For what you are could never be expressed.

You are the space between each breath I take.
The silence that holds every song.

You are the doorway through which the love
Still enters my heart –
The darkness that gives shape to my dreams.

You are the wine that conceals
The sweetness of every day I live
In remembrance of you –
The taste of infinity, and a never-ending joy –

The beauty that trembles
In the shade of every blossom,
And reveals its flower
In the fire of the stars.

Refuge

I travel alone this great highway of Being,
Into the blissful celestial fields
That wait beneath the world.

There I keep company with the Awakened –
The Knowers of Secret Things –
Those who edged in the direction of Eternity,
And never forgot their truth.

They are sane, warm and full of compassion.
They teach of the pathways that lead beyond fear,
Back into the realms of a more authentic nature –

Where every soul is beckoned in its turn
To let go into the sky,
And those vast timeless currents
Upon which they sail –

These Undying Ones,
That send out their unchanging signal
Across all times, eras and places,
To guide every heart to that land they inhabit,
And the wealth of a nation we are yet to discover –

That Kingdom they abide in, both seen and unseen.

Heartland

You could travel the world
In search of the truth.
But you won't find beauty
In the depths of any cave,
Nor love – hiding at the top
Of the highest mountain summit.

If you want to find what's real,
Look into the mirror
Until the mirror falls away –

And recognise
That what you saw
Before this moment,
Is nothing compared
To the translucent light
Of who you truly are.

It's simple, really.
When you look up at the stars,
Just know:
You are face to face
With yourself.

The Way of Love

I'm gathering my strength again –
Trying to remember how this story began,
Though it's easier to forget.

It's true sometimes that I'm falling away,
Like a riptide, cast out from the sea –
Trying to grasp at some kind of understanding –
That final solitary truth that resides
Wherever the fear bows its head,
And the pain is absent.

Relaxing my defences, I take a sip of wine
To awaken my soul to the miracle of this moment,
And everything within it:

The hazy sound of voices
As they echo from the street.
The crow on the rooftop opposite,
Which I have made my friend.
The smell of incense in the air, its smoke
Forming ghostly shapes in the silence.

Sat here alone, on the threshold of eternity,
I have become a witness for my heart –

And in the space between each word
I have used to question myself,
I think that, finally, I have found my answer.

I pause to take a breath
And offer no resistance,
As I step out of the darkness,
At last to meet the light.

Presence

Silence is the sound of everything
Abiding within itself –
A symphony of beauty and truth,
No longer identified with any limitation –

A manifestation of all our desires,
Concentrated into the remembrance
Of the soul's most subtle music –

The sweet song of a nightingale,
Or the rumble of thunder in the night,
That causes us to sense, unexpectedly,
That power from which all things emanate –

The source of love, heard beneath
The running water of a brook,
Deep in the darkest forest –
Returning us to the memory
That in each moment of awareness
We are seated at the edge of forever,
Listening to the voice of creation –

The children of a universe
That came into being
From the most secret point –

A world, eternally held in your mystery –
Now re-made in the image of you.

Appendix: Notes on the Poems

1. **OM** (page 13) – The seed syllable and sacred sound permeating creation, used in meditation to signify the essence of consciousness. In Hinduism, it refers to the Atman (inner-Self) and Brahman (supreme spirit). In Sanskrit, it is the name of the Divine or First Cause, equivalent to the Christian Word – 'In the beginning was the Word, and the Word was with God, and the Word was God.' – *John 1:1*.

2. **'So love, live – / And do with it what you will.'** (page 13) – 'Love and do what you will.' – Saint Augustine of Hippo.

3. **'What recedes in the secret eye gathers the light'** (page 19) – 'The light of the body is the eye: if therefore thine eye be single, thy whole body shall be full of light.' – *Matthew 6:22.*

4. **The Spirit of the Magi** (page 25) – The priestly order of Persia who were the keepers of the world's occult knowledge for centuries. The word 'magic' is derived etymologically from the root 'magi'.

5. **The Stranger** (page 33) – 'Keep thyself as a stranger and a pilgrim upon the earth, to whom

the things of the world appertain not.' – *The Imitation of Christ, The First Book, Chapter XXIII.*

6. **'Like a lark ascending…'** (page 39) – *The Lark Ascending* is a poem by the English poet George Meredith. It inspired the composer Ralph Vaughan Williams to write the popular piece of music by the same name.

7. **'For Rainer'** (page 41) – A dedication to the German modernist poet, Rainer Maria Rilke.

8. **Tanka** (page 45) – A Japanese form of poetry, usually composed of five lines. Traditionally, these poems are about the changing seasons and nature, and the ephemerality of human desires and feelings.

9. **'My stone rolls up and down / An endless hill'** (page 46) – An allusion to the myth of Sisyphus, who was ordered by the gods to roll a boulder up a hill only for it to roll down again every time it neared the top. For trying to cheat Hades, he was cursed to repeat this action for eternity.

10. **Lazarus** (page 48) – A Biblical figure who was raised from the dead by Jesus.

11. **'And we meet, hesitantly in the middle, / Like a lion and a lamb.'** (page 51) – 'And the wolf will dwell with the lamb, and the leopard will lie down with the kid, and the calf and the young lion and the fatling together; and a little boy will lead them.' – *Isaiah 11:6.*

12. **'In uncreated light, / All our stories unite.'** (page 51) – A reference to the mystical Light of Tabor, the Divine Light that was revealed on Mount Tabor at the Transfiguration of Jesus, and was later identified with the same light seen by Saint Paul during his conversion experience on the road to Damascus.

13. **'My contemplative animal says:'** (page 52) – In Aristotelianism, the term 'rational animal' is used as a definition of human nature, which is characterised by its inclination towards logic and reason. To Saint Thomas Aquinas, this reason finds its highest expression in the act of spiritual contemplation, for man is the only creature that has a faculty for mysticism. "It is necessary for the perfection of human society that there should be men who devote their lives to contemplation." — Thomas Aquinas.

14. **'Ecstatic now, / I witness my Bridegroom / Bathed in light.'** (page 56) – An allusion to the mystical marriage of the spiritual adept to

his heavenly counterpart, portrayed erotically as two lovers in the Song of Solomon.

15. **'I saw him and sought him / In the deserts of my soul…'** (page 56) – A reference to the Desert Fathers, the early Christian hermit monks who became the model for devotional monasticism.

16. **Pythia** (page 58) – The Pythia was the name of the high priestess of the Temple of Apollo at Delphi, also known as the Oracle of Delphi. The Temple was thought to be built on a sacred chasm that emitted vapours causing the Pythia to enter various states of delirium and issue prophesies based on her visions. 'Know thyself' is one of the maxims that was said to be inscribed in the forecourt of the Temple.

17. **Rigpa** (page 60) – In Buddhist Dzogchen, Rigpa is presence – the awakened knowledge of the ultimate ground of existence, which is Buddha.

18. **A Felling** (page 63) – 'And now also the axe is laid unto the root of the trees: therefore every tree which bringeth not forth good fruit is hewn down, and cast into the fire.' – *Matthew 3:10.*

19. **'The track that passes all understanding. / The road that does not lead back.'** (page 64) – An homage to thirteenth-century German mystic, Meister Eckhart: 'Whether you like it or not, whether you know it or not, secretly nature seeks, hunts, and tries to ferret out the track on which God may be found.'

20. **'You will know me by my fruits.'** (page 67) – 'Ye shall know them by their fruits. Do men gather grapes of thorns, or figs of thistles?' – *Matthew 7:16.*

21. **For the Asking** (page 69) – 'If grace were always granted immediately and were available for the asking, our weakness could barely sustain it.' – *The Imitation of Christ, The Third Book, Chapter XV.*

22. **'A seed sewn so tightly in an old man's thigh'** (page 90) – A reference to Dionysus, the Greek god of ecstasy and wine, also known as the 'twice born'. After his initial birth, Zeus saved him from death by sewing him up in his thigh and keeping him there until he was ready to be reborn.

23. **'That ageless life in which we are joined, / Darkly…'** (page 92) – 'For now we see in a mirror, darkly…' - *Corinthians 13:12.*

24. **'He joined the Alpha to the Omega'** (page 93) – The Alpha and the Omega are the first and last letters of the Greek alphabet, used to symbolise God and Christ in the Book of Revelation – 'I am the Alpha and the Omega, the First and the Last, the Beginning and the End.' – *Revelation 22:13.*

25. **'Daphne, / Hidden in the leaves of a laurel…'** (page 94) – Daphne is a naiad in Greek mythology, who was transformed into a laurel tree to escape the amorous pursuits of the god Apollo.

26. **Francis** (page 99) – Saint Francis of Assisi, the patron saint of animals and the environment.

27. **Orison** (page 100) – An archaic word for prayer.

28. **'I unveil from sleep the stone of many colours.'** (page 100) – A reference to the Philosopher's Stone, a mythical alchemical substance symbolising perfection, enlightenment and heavenly bliss.

29. **'My green lion takes on wings, / Becomes a fiery dragon.'** (page 100) – In alchemical symbolism, the Green Lion represents man in his undeveloped state. The Lion is hunted

through the forest of the sensual world, and when caught, receives wings to aid it in its flight upwards to the Divine. Finally, the Lion is transmuted into a Red Dragon – a powerful transformation that acts as an allegory for the entire alchemical process, which is driven by the desire to convert the baseness of the human temperament into the elixir of spiritual gold.

30. **'Through seven valleys, my manic soul / Takes flight, like a flock of wild birds, / Dissolving into sky.'** (page 100) – A reference to *The Conference of the Birds*, a long-form poem by the Sufi poet Farid ud-Din Attar. In the poem, the birds must cross seven valleys representing the stages on the path to enlightenment, in order to reach the abode of the legendary Simorgh, a mythical bird symbolic of the Beloved.

31. **'Sinews gently slouching…'** (page 109) – 'And what rough beast, its hour come round at last, / Slouches towards Bethlehem to be born?' – W.B. Yeats, *The Second Coming*.

32. **'And let the stones all speak…'** (page 113) – "I tell you," he replied, "if they keep quiet, the stones will cry out." – *Luke 19:40*.

33. **Saul** (page 121) – The Hebrew name of Saint Paul, a Christian apostle who spread the teachings of Christ in the first century.

34. **'I who had once denied you / Felt the whole length and breadth of Heaven / Breaking behind my eyes.'** (page 122) – 'That Christ may dwell in your hearts by faith; that ye, being rooted and grounded in love, May be able to comprehend with all saints what is the breadth, and length, and depth, and height; And to know the love of Christ, which passeth knowledge, that ye might be filled with all the fulness of God.' – *Ephesians 3: 17-19.*

35. **'They are bathing in living water.'** (page 123) – '"If you knew the gift of God and who it is that asks you for a drink, you would have asked him and he would have given you living water." – *John 4:10.*

36. **'Albion and all her beauty…'** (page 126) – Albion is the earliest known name for Great Britain.

37. **Apotheosis** (page 133) – The highest point in the development of something, the elevation of someone to divine status.

38. **Hope** (page 137) – 'The star of hope. The star of the Magi.' – Samael Aun Weor, *Alchemy and Kabbalah in the Tarot.*

39. **Orpheus** (page 140) – In Greek mythology, the legendary musician and poet who descended into the Underworld of Hades to retrieve his wife, Eurydice.

40. **'We are circles within a circle', they say, / 'With no beginning and never-ending.'** (page 145) – Words adapted from a traditional Pagan saying.

41. **Thoth** (page 148) – The ancient Egyptian god of the moon, wisdom, writing and magic.

42. **Sohbet** (page 160) – In Sufism (mystical Islam), a word indicating a form of spiritual conversation or dialogue.

43. **'Count the cherry stones…'** (page 162) – In English folklore, counting cherry stones is used as an aid in love divination spells.

44. **'Bathe in the adoration / Of the transmutation of the Fifth Ray.'** (page 169) – In esoteric thought, the Seven Rays of Light are the seven waves of energy believed to incarnate the qualities of the Divine. In

Theosophy, the Fifth Initiation (or 'Resurrection') is the level reached by all Masters and Healers prior to their Ascension – human beings that are capable of embodying the Divine.

45. **'The Primal Splendour / Of Colourless Awareness.'** (page 169) – In Buddhism, the realisation of the transparency of awareness conversely reveals the fullness of experience. The traditional Sanskrit word to describe this is Śūnyatā, loosely translated as 'Emptiness'. Śūnyatā denotes both a presence and an absence of self that leads to the non-dual recognition of our inherent Buddha nature. 'Form is emptiness, emptiness is form.' – *The Heart Sutra.*

46. **'In the Scrolls of Akasha – '** (page 170) – In Theosophy, the Akashic Record is a universal compendium chronicling all the events, thoughts, words, emotions and intents that have ever occurred in the past, present and future, for all forms of life. It is believed to exist on the mental plane, where only those with an extrasensory perception can access it.

47. **'Yod. Heh. Vav. Heh.'** (page 171) – The vocalisation of the Tetragrammaton (YHVH), the Hebrew Letters that represent the 'Unutterable Name' of God. In the *Book of*

Exodus 3:13-14, when Moses asks God his name, God simply states 'I Am That I Am.'

48. **'Debating Baudelaire – '** (page 173) – Nineteenth-century French symbolist poet, Charles Baudelaire.

49. **'Eyes open like doves in the wilderness – '** (page 175) – 'Behold, you are beautiful, my love, behold, you are beautiful! Your eyes are doves behind your veil.' – *Song of Songs 4:1*.

50. **Retrograde** (page 186) – The motion of a planet moving in a direction opposite to that of the other bodies in its system. In astrology, this backwards movement is said to affect the normal energy levels and life path of a human being.

51. **Satori & Wine** (page 190) – In Buddhism, Satori is a moment of indescribable enlightenment that arises spontaneously and unexplainedly. In Christianity, wine is used in the celebration of the Eucharistic Communion.

52. **Abraxas** (page 192) – The 'supreme God' of the Basilidians, a Gnostic sect founded in Alexandria in the 2nd century.

53. **Starseed** (page 198) – In New Age belief, Star People are beings who originated as extra-terrestrials before being re-incarnated on Earth.

54. **'In the keeping of our wounds / We have betrayed each other.'** (page 204) – 'And the Lord said unto Cain, Where is Abel thy brother? And he said, I know not: Am I my brother's keeper?' – *Genesis 4:9.*

55. **'Eternity in a grain of sand.'** (page 210) – 'To see a World in a Grain of Sand/ And a Heaven in a Wild Flower / Hold Infinity in the palm of your hand /And Eternity in an hour.' – William Blake, *Auguries of Innocence.*

56. **'With knowledge now of the Kingdom…'** (page 210) – 'How great are His signs! And how mighty are His wonders! His kingdom is an everlasting kingdom, and His dominion is from generation to generation.' – *Daniel 3:33.* Also, 'Thine, O Lord, is the greatness, and the power, and the glory, and the victory, and the majesty; for all that is in the heaven and the earth is Thine; Thine is the kingdom, O Lord, and Thou art exalted as head above all.' – *Chronicles 29:11.*

57. **Drunk** (page 223) – In mystic poetry, wine is often used as a metaphor for spiritual love, representing a state of ecstasy and intoxication outside of the boundaries of the conventional self. 'Drink wine. This is life eternal. This is all that youth will give you. It is the season for wine, roses and drunken friends. Be happy for this moment. This moment is your life.' – Omar Khayyam.

58. **Give Up the Ghost** (page 224) – 'And when Jesus had cried out with a loud voice, he said, Father, into thy hands I commend my spirit: and having said thus, he gave up the ghost.' – *Luke 23:46.*

59. **Samadhi** (page 236) – In Hinduism and Buddhism, the highest state of mental concentration that can be achieved whilst still incarnated in the body, said to unite the meditator with the highest aspect of reality, or Absolute.

60. **'A world, eternally held in your mystery – / Now re-made in the image of you.'** (page 243) – 'So God created mankind in his own image, in the image of God he created them.' – *Genesis 1:27.*

Special Thanks

Special thanks to Adam McKillop, for the striking cover design, and to Stefan Armoneit, for his beautiful, dreamlike artwork. *'The Valley of Unnamed Stars'* is a piece he painted especially inspired by the words in this book, and his art so perfectly matches the spontaneous and mysterious nature of the poems that I can't imagine anything more appropriate. Kindness repays kindness, and I am honoured to have collaborated with two such generous souls, and for their attention and involvement in the evolution of this book.

Thank you to Tim Freke, Shruti Bakshi, John Foster, Samantha SolBright Rodriguez and Rashani Réa, who took the time to read my work in advance and responded with such thoughtful and eloquently written testimonials. Equally, thank you to all my friends and loved ones, who allowed me to share my artistic ambition with them over the years, and whose positive responses gave me the confidence to continue.

And my biggest thank you to Fiona Robertson, who had the eyes to see the spirit at work in my poems, and the heart to help me bring their publication to fruition. This book would not exist in this form if not for the support and encouragement she has given me. She is a true *anam cara*, and words cannot express how grateful I am to her for helping me bring my poetic vision into its full manifestation.

About the Author

C.W. Blackburn is a mystic poet, currently living in Bournemouth, a seaside town on the south coast of England. In 2011, at the age of 24, he started undergoing a series of peak experiences, which led to a gradual shift in his perception from the material to the spiritual. After a return of mental health struggles in his later twenties, he began reading into the wisdom teachings of the major world religions and spiritual traditions, which is the influence and inspiration for his poetry. *Where Words Are Yet To Be Spoken: Poems for Presence* is his first collection.

C.W. Blackburn can be contacted via Sundara Poetry Press at sundarapoetry@gmail.com.

Printed in Great Britain
by Amazon

19799320R00161